Historic Alabama Courthouses

HISTORIC ALABAMA COURTHOUSES

A Century of Their Images and Stories

DELOS HUGHES

NEWSOUTH BOOKS

Montgomery

NewSouth Books
105 S. Court Street
Montgomery, AL 36104

Publisher's Cataloging-in-Publication data

Hughes, Delos
Historic Alabama courthouses : A century of their images and stories / Delos Hughes.
p. cm.

ISBN 978-1-58838-334-1 (paperback)
ISBN 978-1-60306-410-1 (ebook)

1. Courthouses—Alabama. I. Title.

2016958674

Design by Randall Williams

Printed in the United States of America
by Thomson-Shore, Inc.

Contents

Acknowledgments

Acknowledging with a simple list of the many whose contributions made possible a volume of this kind, is clearly inadequate. Nor is it enough to add the truth that it could not have been done without their assistance. Nonetheless, these contributors are mentioned here so that a reader will know that the official "author" did not do it alone. In addition to the individuals and institutions mentioned in the text, a debt of gratitude is owed to: Meredith McDonough of the Alabama Department of Archives and History; John Allison of the Morgan County Archives; the staff of the Auburn University Department of Special Collections and Archives; Jennifer Baughn of the Mississippi Department of Archives and History; Jim Baggett, Don Veasey and Kevin Ray of the Birmingham Public Library; Myra Borden of the Lawrence County Archives; Linda Derry of the Old Cahawba Archeological Park; Kelly Easterling, Chilton County; John E. Enslen, Esq., Wetumpka; James Fuller of the Montgomery County Historical Society; Carolyn Hemstreet of the Hale County Library; Louise Huddleston, Lauderdale County; Stephen M. Kennamer, Esq., Scottsboro; Kathy Marko of the Cherokee County Museum; John P. Oliver, Esq., Dadeville; Stephanie Rogers and Jane Ellen Clark (formerly) of the Monroe County Heritage Museum; Bobby Joe Seales of the Shelby County Historical Society; Emily Sparrow, Auburn; John Stevenson, editor, *Randolph County Leader*; Gayle Thomas of the Henry County Historical Group, Inc.; Ken Thomas, Atlanta, Georgia: John T. Thornhill of the Clay County Historical Society; Mary Paluzzi and Marina Klarik of the University of Alabama Records Management and Archives; Sheila Ward of the Coosa County Historical Society; Elizabeth Teaff and Laura Hewett of the Washington and Lee University Library; Ellen Weiss, New Orleans, Louisiana; Sally Wiant of the Washington and Lee University School of Law; Joan Spann Williams of the Cherokee County Public Library.

I mention separately Keith Vincent, whose website, *CourthouseHistory*, is an invaluable storehouse for postcard images of courthouses. His generosity in providing information about them and permitting me to use some of those images in this volume is remembered with gratitude.

Above all, I am indebted to my friend and mentor, Robert Gamble, who knows, I believe, as much about Alabama architecture as everyone else put together, and whose willingness to share his knowledge and careful judgment is the background for whatever merit readers may find in these pages but responsible for none of whatever mistakes, misjudgments or ill-advised barbs have slipped into them.

HISTORIC ALABAMA COURTHOUSES

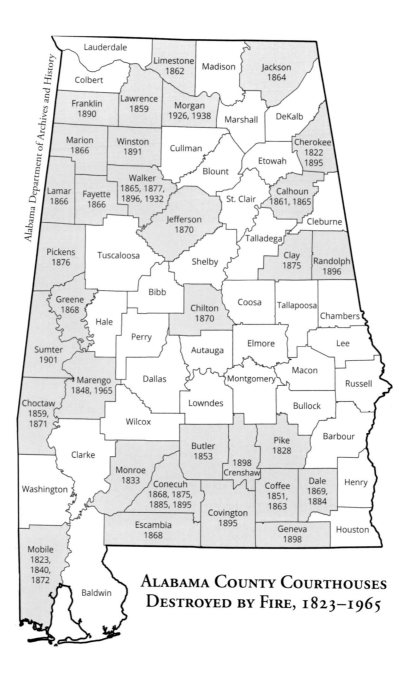

Lauderdale

Limestone
1862

Madison

Jackson
1864

Colbert

Franklin
1890

Lawrence
1859

Morgan
1926, 1938

DeKalb

Marshall

Marion
1866

Winston
1891

Cullman

Cherokee
1822
1895

Etowah

Walker
1865, 1877,
1896, 1932

Blount

Lamar
1866

Fayette
1866

St. Clair

Calhoun
1861, 1865

Jefferson
1870

Cleburne

Talladega

Pickens
1876

Tuscaloosa

Shelby

Clay
1875

Randolph
1896

Bibb

Greene
1868

Coosa

Tallapoosa

Chambers

Hale

Chilton
1870

Perry

Elmore

Lee

Sumter
1901

Autauga

Marengo
1848, 1965

Dallas

Montgomery

Macon

Russell

Choctaw
1859,
1871

Lowndes

Bullock

Wilcox

Clarke

Butler
1853

Pike
1828

Barbour

Monroe
1833

1898
Crenshaw

Washington

Conecuh
1868, 1875,
1885, 1895

Coffee
1851,
1863

Dale
1869,
1884

Henry

Covington
1895

Escambia
1868

Geneva
1898

Houston

Mobile
1823,
1840,
1872

Baldwin

ALABAMA COUNTY COURTHOUSES
DESTROYED BY FIRE, 1823–1965

Note: All counties and cities mentioned in this book are in Alabama unless otherwise indicated.

An Introduction

Utilitas, Firmitas, Venustas

The Roman architect Vitruvius knew nothing about Alabama's county courthouses, but he had strong opinions about the qualities of fine architecture. The standards for judging architecture according to him are **commodity**, *firmness*, and **delight**. That is, an admirable building must serve the purpose for which it is built; it must stand securely, unthreatened by dangers above or catastrophes below; and it must please the senses, sight above all. One way to understand the development of county courthouse types in Alabama, the subject of this volume, is by noting that an order to the Vitruvian criteria guides the process. Early on, "commodity" principally guides the design and building process. Later, "firmness" is added. Later still, "delight" joins the other two.

Commodity. To begin with the obvious, courts do not need "houses" at all. Whatever business courts convene to transact may be conducted in open air in almost any unimproved setting. If Mark Hopkins seated on one end of a log and his student on the other end is an apt image for education, we can easily imagine a court convening in similarly primitive settings even with a full complement of participants—judge, jury, litigants, public. It is reported that at Wedowee, court sessions for Randolph County were held in open air until 1836.[1] But shelter is sometimes necessary—in poor weather, certainly—and frequently desirable. Neither necessity nor desirability, however, requires a specialized shelter, that is, a *courthouse*. Indeed, in the early history of many American counties the first courts convened in private homes, stores, taverns, and inns. The community understood these to be temporary accommodations; they were, in fact, succeeded more or less quickly by purpose-built courthouses.

Replacing an *ad hoc* courthouse with a dedicated building provided several advantages. On private property, a householder or proprietor might be at an unfair advantage in proceedings involving himself. A public building on public property removed at least the appearance of such impropriety. Further, because courts held in homes, inns, taverns, and such were at the mercy of the property

1. Donna J. Sieben-thaler, "Randolph County," *Encyclopedia of Alabama.*

3

2. Benj. B. Smith to Hon. Zell Gaston, Judge of Probate, Butler County, 11 March 1903. Reported in *Greenville Advocate*, 18 March 1903.

owners' whims, resulting changes of fees or court locations were problematic for the smooth conduct of the public's legal business. More important than these considerations was a common understanding that the proper conduct of court business required a specialized setting. English Common Law traditions, adopted and adapted by American legal custom, required a particular arrangement of courtrooms that private houses and taverns were ill-suited to provide. In addition, over time counties needed larger and larger facilities to store public records, juries required security and privacy during deliberations, and lawyers demanded more space to spread their documents and exhibits before the court—all parts of the rationale for erecting a purpose-built courthouse in a fixed location in a county.

Firmness. As Alabama moved from territorial to state governance, the Legislature, newly organized in 1819, imposed upon counties the obligation to provide their citizens with a set of public facilities, namely a jail, stocks, and a courthouse. The expense was to be borne by the citizens of the county. Not surprisingly, county authorities turned to whatever materials were at hand and typically put up their first courthouses with scant attention to Vitruvius's emphasis on *firmness.* The early log or frame courthouse buildings were NOT very firm. But neither were they expected to be the permanent seats of justice for their counties. Of the vintage courthouses pictured in the pages that follow, only a few frame buildings (and thus few photographs of them) have survived, the Washington County courthouse being the earliest and most familiar.

Firmness was very much on the minds of county authorities when the original county buildings became so dilapidated as to require replacing because they were uncomfortable or even dangerous, or just simply beyond repair. County authorities sometimes called in experts to assess problematic conditions of their courthouses. This report from the Montgomery architect, B. B. Smith, was not an unusual one, even considering that Mr. Smith may have had a vested interest in claiming that the building he was assessing needed to be replaced. Of the 1871 Butler County courthouse he reported:

> Foundations, especially at the corners are very rotten; mortar has entirely disintegrated and bricks have deteriorated until they are worthless. The entire building is in very bad condition, mortar throughout worthless, brick soft; relieving arches over windows in many cases broken and walls badly cracked.
>
> The ends of the joists on second floor have dry rotted until I do not hesitate to say that it is very dangerous to put a large crowd in the court room. In fact this floor is altogether unsafe.[2]

It is the responsibility of county grand juries in Alabama to report the condition of county buildings. In Autauga County, persistent charges to grand juries referred to the poor condition of the nineteenth-century courthouse. In response, one grand jury reported "the court house in bad shape, as the foundation was rotten and the building scarcely safe." By then, resources in Autauga and many other counties were ample or reliable enough to afford a "permanent" courthouse. None of these "second-wave" buildings was log; few were frame; the material of choice was masonry, usually brick, rarely stone. Planning for these buildings was minimal, seldom professional. County authorities usually chose a local builder without competition, stipulated very general requirements, and provided minimal plan details and only occasionally style preferences. In a few instances, instructions from the county suggested copying a building in a nearby county. But the general pattern was that the builder was also the designer of the building. As these more elaborate courthouses required a substantial financial commitment from the county—whether in monies already collected or in future revenues through bond issues—a performance bond became a regular part of a builder's contract with the county, to insure that he completed the project, did so on time, and followed whatever specifications the county courthouse building committee had provided.

In pursuit of "firmness," a typical specification gave particular attention to fireproofing the courthouse building. Just as in Autauga, the danger of courthouse fires was on the minds of Alabama's county authorities, for many log and frame courthouses, and even some brick ones, had been lost to fire.[3] The Alabama Department of Archives and History has prepared a map (see page 2) of county courthouses destroyed by fire—sometimes more than once—showing how prevalent such catastrophes were.[4]

Arson by disgruntled defendants and petitioners hoping to delay court proceedings or destroy records was frequently suspected. Yet carelessly managed heating equipment and procedures were more likely the actual causes of destruction by fire. Masonry construction was the first response to the problem, yet even masonry buildings sometimes went up in flames because their roofs, floors, and furnishings were still flammable and vulnerable. Not until steel and concrete were introduced into courthouse construction was a requirement that the construction be "fireproof" common in courthouse building contracts.

Delight. Though as the state matured, Alabamians usually considered the condition of their courthouses in terms of utility and soundness, in early days they did not often acclaim their beauty nor defend their handsomeness. But as the frontier qualities of the state began to fade, control of public decisions in counties came to lodge more and more firmly in the hands of those who could

3. See *Prattville Progress*, 25 March 1904, for report of grand jury regarding dilapidation of courthouse and danger of losing county records to fire. Butler County authorities' response to the danger of fire was typical in specifying that contractors bid for a "building to be of brick covered with fireproof materials." Butler County Commissioners' Court, *Minutes 1860–1871,* commissioners meeting for May 1870, p. 442.

4. Alabama Department of Archives and History, http://www.archives.state.al.us/referenc/images/firemap.gif.

5. A common pattern in disputes over courthouse building projects pitted in-town citizens against country dwellers. Larger landholders typically complained that they would bear most of the costs of a new building, while the business community argued that a new courthouse was an investment that would increase population, business, and tax revenues to (over time) pay for the building. See, for example, the 1902–04 debate recorded in editorials and letters-to-the-editor in the *Monroe Journal* concerning building the Monroe County courthouse.

afford the time and wherewithal to devote to politics. These elites, such as they were, paid increasing attention to style, as do stylish elites nearly everywhere. Their pronounced attachment to Classical Revival style meant that those patterns soon appeared in courthouses no less than in dwellings and churches and schools and commercial buildings. The classical revival was *de rigueur* in antebellum Alabama and survived with some vigor in post-Civil War years. However, as an entrepreneurial class developed in Alabama in the Reconstruction era, one of the many challenges it laid down to the old order concerned architectural taste. When county authority shifted to men who embraced the philosophy of the "New South" movement, courthouse building committees were increasingly likely to look to the more up-to-date, sometimes bizarre, often eclectic architectural ideas of professional architects.[5] "Boosterism" in the reviving southern states demanded county symbols, courthouses in particular, that beckoned newcomers and investors with evidence—in transportation, journalism, and architecture—of new and promising opportunities within sight and sound of the courthouse bell tower.

Catering to the growing demand for something new and different from the older classical revival was a growing class of courthouse architects. The names of Alexander Bruce, Andrew J. Bryan, Walter Chamberlin, James W. Golucke, Edward C. Hosford, Frank Milburn, and P. H. Weathers, are attached to many such courthouses (as well as a few neoclassical ones) across the states of the old South.

ON THE PAGES FOLLOWING are photographs—and a brief text about each image—of courthouses built in Alabama at least one hundred years ago. Some of the buildings still stand; most do not. Necessarily, these are not *all* of the courthouses in Alabama built at least one hundred years ago; no photographs have been located for numbers of others described in county records. The collection is presented alphabetically and within counties chronologically. Most of the included photographs are the earliest found, to show the original intentions of those who created the courthouse as nearly as possible.

Two observations of special interest to the author will be found in several of the text passages. One is the extent to which county courthouse designs are based on those of existing courthouses, sometimes literally copied. A familiar assumption of those who study and write about early courthouses is that these structures express some quality unique to the community that the building served. "Similarity" and "imitation" suggest that the qualities may not be unique or at least that a much deeper level of analysis is required to sort out what the building reveals about the community.

The second observation that a reader will notice in the textual passages is the influence of South Carolina's courthouse tradition on Alabama's (and many other states') early courthouses. The literal independence of administrative and judicial spaces—that is, no access to second-floor court facilities without exiting the building and reentering up exterior stairs—is difficult to understand for reasons of economy or convenience. While the arrangement did express certain values of separation of powers in South Carolina history, no such history nor any such actual separation of powers ever existed to be expressed at the county level in Alabama. This author's conclusion is that the explanation is aesthetic, and the taste for building in this fashion is greatly influenced by the emigration into Alabama by South Carolinians and the influence they had on their descendants. The director of the 1880 United States Census reported to the Congress that "from 1820 to 1860 South Carolina was a bee-hive, from which swarms were continually going forth to populate the newer cotton-growing states of the Southwest."[6] The South Carolina influence is especially noticeable across the Alabama Black Belt, for that is where emigrants from South Carolina often discovered the rich cotton soils they had come to find. In the northern part of the state, on the other hand, types of design and cultural preferences were more likely to have arrived by emigration routes through Tennessee, from the Upper South and Ohio Valley.

That the courthouse history of any county in any state is a continuing source of interest to a wide audience may be judged from the steady appearance of books and articles devoted to such stories. That may be because so many of the factors that make up any community are part of that history—not just its taste in architecture, but also the history of its politics, its economy, its socioeconomic character, its ethnic make-up. This record of a part of that history in Alabama has included just part of these buildings. The exterior—the facades, the elevations, the surface materials, the locations and sites and sizes—the public face, may be the most revealing source of information about the community. The interior, how the building is arranged, the relationship of its parts, the ways it is used and for what, can reveal still more. However, that exploration is for another book.

6. Francis A. Walker, *Compendium of the Tenth Census (June 1, 1880)*, "Introduction," lxiii.

AUTAUGA COUNTY COURTHOUSE, PRATTVILLE (1870)

Architect and Builder: George Littlefield Smith

Histories record that Prattville was not the first "permanent" county seat of Autauga, but the third. Nor was the building pictured here the first "permanent" courthouse. It was probably the second, but not the last. The Autauga county seat moved from Washington (now "Old Washington") where, reportedly, a brick courthouse was built, to Kingston, and in 1868 to Prattville, the up-and-coming manufacturing and population center of the county though not at all its geographical center. In Prattville, George Littlefield Smith planned and built this two-story courthouse. The interior was conventional with county offices below and courtroom fitted out with a gallery above. To the exterior, however, Smith gave Italianate pretensions—paired brackets under the roof, a pilaster under each pair defining three bays of the gabled Court Street end and seven on the longer side, plus bracketed hoods above the front and side entrances. Smith, whose own home is one of the centerpieces of the historical district of Prattville, finished the building in 1870. His fellow townsman, Prattville's most eminent citizen, Daniel Pratt, may have had some hand in planning or executing the building plan, for this native New Englander came to the area not just with industrial ambitions but with architectural credentials as well.

This first courthouse in Prattville served the county from 1870 until 1906 when the second one was built several blocks north on Court Street. Since 1906, the building has passed to several private owners for uses as varied as a cement block manufactory, an automobile dealership and service station (from an addition to its street side), liquor store, retail shops, warehouse, church, and dance studio.

NEW COURT HOUSE, PRATTVILLE, ALA.

Keith Vincent, *CourthouseHistory*

AUTAUGA COUNTY COURTHOUSE, PRATTVILLE (1906)

Architect: Bruce Architectural Company; Builder: M. T. Lewman & Company

Atlanta-based Bruce Architectural Company established a satellite office in Birmingham, hoping to broaden its reach beyond Georgia. Its foresight was rewarded in Prattville with a contract to design a new courthouse replacing the outmoded 1870 structure. The building's more-or-less Richardsonian Romanesque character is a statement of Autauga ambition more than of Autauga necessity. "Wide awake and progressive Prattville," the *Prattville Progress* trumpeted, "whose streets are already decorated with many modern structures, is justly proud of this new temple of justice, which will stand a prominent mile post, showing the rapid strides along the road of progress which our county is making."

The plan of the building is bilaterally symmetrical, but has an appearance of irregularity due to the varying heights of projecting corner towers. Fire insurance maps for the building note that only the exterior is fireproof and that the roof is laid on steel trusses. The efficient Louisville-based contractor, M. T. Lewman & Co., which previously had built a similar Bruce-designed courthouse in Georgia, faced delays from materials shortages and striking workers but brought the building in on time and on budget, at a cost to the county of $44,000.

Old Methodist Church Museum of Daphne

BALDWIN COUNTY COURTHOUSE, DAPHNE (1888)

Architect: Rudolph Benz; Builder: Robert Voltz

After the Baldwin County seat was moved from Blakeley and before it was moved again to Bay Minette, the county courthouse was located in Daphne. Mobile architect Rudolph Benz produced a cube of a building that served the county for more than thirty years, and afterwards had a second life as a school building. The architect gave it features that seem whimsical but admittedly relieve a certain stolidity in the underlying mass. Gables are centered on all four sides of the mansard or deck roof. The front elevation shows three bays, featuring in the center bay an elaborately decorated gable, a doorway with semi-circular transom surrounded by decorative brickwork on the second floor, and a first-floor portico topped by decorative railing around the balcony accessed from the second-floor doorway. Pierced brick pilasters ornament the corners and sides of the building and string and belt courses provide horizontal interest that is capped by a finely executed crown of brick at the roofline.

University of South Alabama

BALDWIN COUNTY COURTHOUSE, BAY MINETTE (1901)

Architect: Lockwood & Smith; Builder: F. M. Dobson

An oft-told story in Baldwin County is that after the Alabama Legislature authorized moving the county seat from Daphne to Bay Minette, the reluctance of Daphne officials to give up county records led to a midnight raid to rescue the records and deliver them to Bay Minette. An all-star cast had produced the courthouse that became their depository. Frank Lockwood and Benjamin Bosworth Smith, two of Alabama's best known, respected, and prolific architects of their day, were briefly partners in producing this and other courthouses before resuming independent practices. Francis Dobson, field agent for Lockwood & Smith, sometimes negotiated contracts for the firm and in Baldwin County was building supervisor on the courthouse project. Lockwood's popularity was in part due to his versatility. The Romanesque Revival style (here with an entrance through a Syrian arch) of the Bay Minette courthouse was but one of the modes he produced according to his clients' tastes. In Baldwin County it conveyed permanence, stability, seriousness—just the message that Bay Minette wanted to convey following a contested removal of the county seat.

Keith Vincent, *Courthouse History*

BARBOUR COUNTY COURTHOUSE, CLAYTON (1852)

Architect: Unrecorded; Builder: Unrecorded

Barbour County, one of three in Alabama that has two county seats (Barbour, Coffee, St. Clair), built its first courthouse of logs in Clayton, centrally located in the county. The first "permanent" courthouse was an 1854 structure, pictured above after being remodeled in 1900 to satisfy the then current taste for classical style. Regrettably the county records that would allow a fuller understanding of how the building originally appeared have been misplaced. Early Sanborn maps show that instead of the classical portico over the main entrance, the original entry to the second story was by a double curved stairway, also providing shelter for the entrance to the first floor. This feature points to the influence in courthouse style of South Carolina forms and, indeed, the earliest pioneers in the area, the Williams family for whom the first settlement, nearby Williamstown, was named, were South Carolinians. The missing early county records almost certainly name the building's contractor but no other records and no newspapers have been found with that information. The remodeling of 1900 included adding the columned portico and clock dome. In 1924, wings were added. The building was replaced on the same site by the 1961 courthouse of modern design.

The Barbour County courthouse in Eufaula was located in a building that included the Eufaula City Hall as well. No photographs have yet been found showing this 1878 structure that is attributed to M. D. Britt and Daniel as architects and builders. Like the 1852 Clayton courthouse, this building in Eufaula featured a double exterior stair that is described in contemporaneous accounts and drawn on Sanborn Fire Insurance Co. maps.

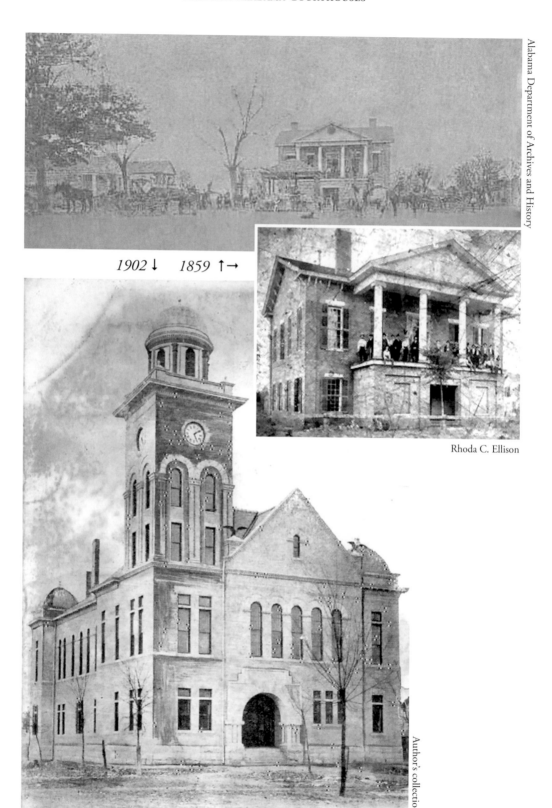

1902 ↓   *1859* ↑→

Rhoda C. Ellison

BIBB COUNTY COURTHOUSES, CENTREVILLE (1859) (1902)

1859: Architect: Unrecorded; Builder: C. A. Shelby

The small well-proportioned building that C. A. Shelby constructed as the third Bibb County courthouse fits exactly into the pattern of courthouse evolution from log to frame to brick—in this case providing some unexpected "delights" in the portico, along with conventional ones in the brackets under the eaves. The building—as with a number of other Alabama courthouses—gives a literal expression to the institutional "separation of powers," allowing judicial functions to occupy a separate floor having separate entrances from the portico. The symbolism, however, is entirely gratuitous as Alabama counties never were allowed an independent judicial function (nor executive, nor legislative), being since the state's origin under the thumb of the state legislature.

Nonetheless the portico is an admirable architectural accomplishment. Though the columns are quite expectable, their Ionic capitals are a more sophisticated touch than one might expect in rural Alabama county courthouses, especially since the Ionic used is the Scamozzi version, so that the volutes appear the same from any side. The building overall mixes stylistic elements –the classicism of the portico with the Italianate bracketed eaves— that may be found in several late antebellum courthouses in Alabama, as in Lauderdale and Wilcox counties (*q.v.*). The entrance under the portico was also well designed, not alone for the receding panels worked into the brick, but also for protecting the stairs (not observable in this photograph) to the second floor entrance. Maintenance of exterior stairs has proved a continuing headache for courthouses nearly everywhere. Though less problematic in Alabama's clement weather than in more rigorous climates, relocating stairs to second floors is often a major renovation move (e.g., in Barbour County, *q.v.*).

1902: Architect: William S. Hull; Builder: F. M. Dobson

Befitting its post-Reconstruction era ambitions, Bibb County looked beyond Old South style and beyond local talent to produce its fourth, expanded courthouse in 1902. W. S. Hull was one of Jackson, Mississippi's experienced Hull Brothers (William S. was architect, Frank B. was contractor) who had designed and built courthouses widely in the southeastern region. The builder in Centreville, F. M. Dobson & Co. of Montgomery, was an important contractor for public buildings, especially jails (in Geneva County, for example). The building design was eye-opening for the time and place. The main entrance owes something to Richardsonian style and the general impression tends toward the Romanesque. Although the elevations, with the dominating corner clock/bell tower, may appear otherwise, in plan the ochre brick building is symmetrical. Corner domes all around are a further unexpected feature. Overall, the building conveys an impression more ecclesiastical than governmental or administrative or political.

Oneonta Public Library

BLOUNT COUNTY COURTHOUSE, BLOUNTSVILLE (1888)

Architect and Builder: Otto Puls

To forestall an imminent move of the county seat to Oneonta, Blountsville authorities built a new courthouse, shown here, to replace the dilapidated building that since 1833 had served Blount County. The ploy was unsuccessful; county offices and county records moved to Oneonta in 1889, even though at the time it had no courthouse at all. Otto Puls was given the contract to build the Blountsville courthouse that he also designed, for $16,200. Puls, a German immigrant who had first settled in Chicago to work in rebuilding that city after its great fire, had later come to Alabama where he established a reputation as a builder of covered bridges (one near Oneonta, see *infra*, and another in Lee County still exist). In Blount County, he was not, apparently, a partisan in the rivalry between Blountsville and Oneonta over the location of the county seat, for he secured courthouse contracts in both places.

Oneonta Public Library

Blount County Courthouse, Oneonta (1890)

Architect and Builder: Otto W. Puls

The two Oneonta structures known to have been designed and built by the local contractor, Otto Puls—the Easley Covered Bridge and the Blount County courthouse—are both service-able and quite ordinary architecturally. The somber red brick courthouse offers little of the stylishness that boosters of more progressive counties of the time insisted their courthouses feature in order to appear up-to-date and thereby attract newcomers and investment. Entrance to the building's first floor of offices is through a semi-enclosed vestibule and under the stair leading to the upper-floor courtroom. A prominent dormer pierces the front of the steeply pitched roof, and a "schoolyard-type" bell tower crowns its peak. Indeed, the whole building resembles a country school more than a county courthouse. In 1906, the Supreme Court of Alabama decided in an unusual case (*Parker et al. v. Blount County,* 148 Ala. 275) that the safe used for records storage that the county had installed several years after the building was completed, was *not* part of the building that Blount County later sold, and that the county retained ownership of the safe even though not of the building!

BULLOCK COUNTY COURTHOUSE, UNION SPRINGS (1872)

Architect and Builder: M. M. Tye

The fashionable Second Empire style arrived on the Alabama courthouse scene in the appearance of the 1872 Bullock County courthouse in Union Springs. The much-altered Coosa County courthouse (*q.v.*) is said to have originally displayed the style though its alterations have made that difficult to confirm. The Bullock County design is attributed to M. M. Tye, a versatile and popular regional builder who is credited with other area courthouses (e.g., Dale County) and homes. The principal façade of his Bullock County courthouse shows he was not a stylistic purist, but was inclined to include some idiosyncratic touches to the Second Empire vocabulary, such as fanlighted doors and an incongruous cast-iron gallery on the second floor. Tye must have been well connected to suppliers of the (probably metal) architectural embellishments that lend such a vivid appearance to the building. Its twin corner pavilions with swooping mansard roofs dominate the streetscape, making the courthouse an unforgettable architectural standout among its neighbors.

Greenville Weekly Advocate

BUTLER COUNTY COURTHOUSE, GREENVILLE (1871)

Architect: Unrecorded; Builder: D. T. McCall and M. Wimberly

Though the name of the architect of the 1871 Butler County courthouse is presently unknown, the South Carolina heritage of its style seems clear, and is not surprising given the birthplaces of many of the earliest settlers around the county seat of Greenville or Buttsville as it once was known. The building stood on the site of two previous frame court buildings, the immediate predecessor planned by local resident A. G. Smith and John K. Hardy and built by local contractor Brockman W. Henderson. Mindful of the fire that destroyed Butler County's courthouse in 1853, and of the cramped quarters of the small courthouse that replaced it, Butler decided in 1870 to build in brick and to provide space for seven offices on the ground floor, entered off a commodious 10-foot wide corridor. The second floor provided a large courtroom, judge's chamber, and jury room.

The most arresting feature of the exterior was the wide-reaching double curved stair leading to the second floor portico with modest columns that is the entrance to the courtroom. Between the flights of stairs was an open entryway under a segmental arch to the ground floor flanked by narrow niches with semicircular arches. The front-facing gable, rendered as a pediment, contained a circular window into the attic space. Brackets under the eaves and pediment completed this pleasing, well-proportioned architectural ensemble.

BUTLER COUNTY COURTHOUSE, GREENVILLE (1904)

Architect: B. B. Smith; Builder: Dobson & Bynum

Like many other Alabama counties, Butler entered the twentieth century with a new vision of what the county should be, a vision requiring a new aesthetic in its most prominent public building. Officially the deterioration of the 1871 courthouse (including its roof blown off by hurricane winds in 1901) and the high cost of restoring it were the reasons offered for building a new courthouse. The new design owed nothing to South Carolina precedents, little to Old South style. It was—for the time—thoroughly modern, quite complicated in plan, and calculated to be a landmark with its soaring central clock and bell tower. This was a building for boosters and entrepreneurs, of which Butler County had a generous supply and hopes for many more.

While the first-floor plan included only six offices, the second floor was larger than most courthouses in rural Alabama counties, having spectator balconies along each side of the courtroom, four jury rooms, and a commodious space for a judge. But, whether intended from the first or not, office suites inserted into basement and attic spaces conveniently accommodated Butler County's growth and the expanding reach of county and state government.

The footprint of the building is notable, though not unique, for the many 135 degree angles that compose it. Centered on the side walls of the major (front) block are three-sided bays. At the rear corners of the minor block are octagonal projections, topped above the second floor by conical rooflets. Both bays and rear projections are fitted with windows on both floors. Just as he had done in Bibb County, contractor F. M. Dobson, here in partnership with B. C. Bynum, created an appropriate expression of the optimism and ambitions of another New South community.

Alabama Department of Archives and History

Calhoun County Courthouse, Jacksonville (1886)

Architect: Unrecorded; Builder: J. B. Patton

Following the customary sequence of courthouses of log, then frame, then brick, Calhoun authorities built a brick courthouse on the Jacksonville town square. In 1886, in part to stave off the ultimately successful efforts to move the county seat to Anniston—which enthusiastic locals had dubbed the "Model City of the New South"—county authorities built another, more substantial brick courthouse. The earlier one was razed; since, the square has remained open. Though not pretentious, the 1886 structure was not without interesting architectural features. Brackets under the eaves and the semi-circular window arches were conventional embellishments to even modest public buildings. But it was the assembled vertical elements that drew attention upward from elaborate front-door detailing past the pedimented second-floor projection to the unusual cupola. That structure itself was composed of distinctive elements: a square platform below a convex roof, with a single front-facing dormer in classical style, upon which rose a square enclosure providing four clock faces, and above that a smaller roof section that reproduced the curves of the lower one, projecting over and thus protecting the clock dials, and, finally, a finial drawing the whole assembly to a point.

Upon removal of the county seat to Anniston in 1900, the building was incorporated into the Jacksonville Normal School (now Jacksonville State University), but was later demolished.

CALHOUN COUNTY COURTHOUSE
—ANNISTON, ALA.

CALHOUN COUNTY COURTHOUSE, ANNISTON (1902)

Architect: J. W. Golucke; Builder: S. C. Houser and T. C. Wolsoncroft

To the Calhoun County Building Committee in 1901, architect James W. Golucke presented a far more conventional New South courthouse design than those that Bibb and Butler counties had adopted. A prolific designer of courthouses (some twenty-seven by one count), Atlanta's Golucke produced many variations of the style in the years before his tragic imprisonment, attempted suicide, and finally death of gastritis in 1907. The Calhoun County courthouse defies confident description of its style. Some have called it "Neo-Classical Revival," referring to exterior decorations and symmetry of the plan. Perhaps "Renaissance Revival" would do as well to call attention to the rusticated base and the *piano nobile* second floor. Golucke designed neither the projecting porticoes nor the recessed loggias of the Anniston building with full-height columns, as usually was found in Neoclassical Revival facades. Instead, the lower portion of each of the Corinthian entry features was faced with an arcade, a widely used motif in American courthouses and with European precedents.

At each corner of the roof stood a miniature version of its towering center dome. In later Golucke designs, the inevitable central dome became wider and wider to eventually fill nearly the width of the courthouse roof (*e.g.*, the "rectangular dome" atop the Morgan County courthouse in Madison, Georgia). The Anniston building was large enough that the second floor is not entirely occupied by one courtroom, as in most other courthouses up to this time. That also allowed the center of the first-floor lobby to include a well under the dome so that light penetrated through the whole height. The building has been altered several times; many original features have disappeared, notably the dome, now replaced by a slender square clock tower.

Don Clark

CHAMBERS COUNTY COURTHOUSE, LaFAYETTE (1837)

Architect: Thomas C. Russell (Courthouse Commissioner);
Builder: Joshua S. Mitchell and Benjamin H. Cameron

To an untrained eye, little about the 1837 Chambers County courthouse may seem stylish. Yet the surviving contract for the building records a careful attention to detail, so a closer look is required. A more discerning examination finds here a robust expression of Federal style simplicity, including a full entablature, semi-elliptical transoms over doorways, pedimented gables and the unusually canted bulls-eye openings in the main gable. With only a few differences, the courthouse that Benjamin Cameron had earlier built for Troup County, Georgia, was the model for this one. The design also intrigues historians because it so closely resembles the Dallas County courthouse built in Cahawba for which no recorded connection with builders Mitchell and Cameron has yet been found. Except for the side gable shown above, the buildings seem identical, even down to the unusual angle at which twin oval openings were set into the end pediments. In addition, the 1837 Chambers County is at least a close cousin to the Tallapoosa County courthouse of 1839 (*q.v.*) by the same builders.

Wide halls divided the ground floor of the 40'x 60' Chambers County building into four equal offices each entered from the halls on two sides. In imitation of the Troup County building, the second floor was finely finished with an ensemble of judge's seat, jury boxes, and bar that together composed a circular arrangement at the business end of the courtroom. A concern for the security of the two jury rooms facing the judge from the rear of the space was indicated by specifications for locks on their doors and shutters on their windows.

CHAMBERS COUNTY COURTHOUSE, LaFAYETTE (1900)

Architect: Golucke & Stewart; Builder: Philip Yeager

Looking closely at both Chambers County courthouses pictured here and *supra* should be sufficient warning against reading too much about the distinctive qualities of communities from characteristics of their public buildings. If the 1837 courthouse is a near duplicate of the Troup County building (and perhaps other courthouses as well), the 1900 courthouse is at least a close cousin of the Calhoun County courthouse of 1902, unsurprising as both were designed by James W. Golucke. To appear progressive by adopting a fashionable style and hiring a popular architect was apparently more important to some Alabama counties than was expressing in their public architecture anything unique about themselves.

The restoration of this building (and an addition to it) in 2003 was attended with extensive publicity complimenting its careful preservation. In this building and in most of this era, the courtroom no longer occupied the entire upper floor. In Chambers County, only half of that floor belongs to the courtroom and associated judicial spaces, the rest for administrative offices that previously would have been confined to the first floor. A great deal of the space on the first floor is devoted to the circular center vestibule, open through the second floor and to the dome, and to an impressive double flight of stairs to the second floor.

Golucke highlighted the design with eye-catching white-work to set elements off from the dark brick mass of the building. The arched entry openings, the window hoods that march aggressively across the second level and around the drum of the done, and even the white horizontals of foundation, belt course, and dome base, all invite the eye to play over the surfaces of the building and recognize that it is of more than ordinary importance.

Cherokee County Public Library

CHEROKEE COUNTY COURTHOUSE, CENTRE (1896)

Architect: Unrecorded; Builder: T. L. Houser & T. C. Wolsoncroft

It is perplexing today to understand how nineteenth -century surveyors located the "geographic center of a county" as the Alabama Legislature ordered be done for Cherokee County following an alteration of its boundaries. While today that *centroid* can be identified with modern mapping and computer techniques, the commission charged with that responsibility in 1844 in Cherokee County had no such tools, yet reported a finding. Around the frame courthouse that county authorities quickly built there, the town appropriately named Centre commenced to grow. After five more years, a brick courthouse replaced the earlier one. Fire consumed it in 1882 and its successor in 1895. The more durable courthouse of 1896, pictured here, lived for forty years. Houser and Wolsoncroft had enlarged the original building in 1900.

Befitting a facility so prone to burning, the commanding architectural feature is a bell tower that might alert citizens of any further fire danger. No clock is observable in the tower; presumably there was none. As to architectural style, "eclectic" seems to work best. A bulbous Second Empire style tower roof oversees a diverse collection of elements below. A centered projection with corner pilasters includes a tripartite window with semicircular arches above the first-floor entrance door. The entrance itself is ornamented with a segmental arch, narrow flanking windows with lights in decorative shapes, and quoins beside them at the corners of the projection.

Chilton-Clanton Public Library

CHILTON COUNTY COURTHOUSE, CLANTON (1872)

Architect: Unrecorded; Builder: Alexander G. Dake & John Grant

When the Chilton County (once Baker County) seat moved from Grantville and abandoned its log first courthouse, a frame building in Clanton succeeded it. But for its odd portico, this 1872 structure might be thought to have originally been an imposing antebellum residence. Although quite plain, from this surviving photograph, it appears to have been finely built and finished even though without an entablature, with broad end chimneys and shuttered nine-over-nine windows. The entrance through the portico was fitted out with side and transom glass. What was concealed within the weatherboarded lower floor of the portico, one may guess, might be small office spaces or, more likely, stairs to a second floor courtroom. The generous dimensions of the open second floor of the portico suggest its use for public pronouncements, and addresses on public occasions. Although it had an attractive railing in front, its sides were simply weatherboard up to railing height. No explanation has survived.

One A. J. Cooper, who had built an earlier Chilton County courthouse at Grantville, was initially awarded the contract to build the 1872 courthouse. As he was a county commissioner at the time of the award, he had to give up the contract which was then awarded to Alexander Dake. The Dakes were prominent and early Chilton Countians, who filled many public offices for the county as well as for the town of Clanton. Whether either Alexander Dake or his nephew John Grant were professional builders or were simply supervising contractors is not clear.

Keith Vincent, *CourthouseHistory*

CHILTON COUNTY COURTHOUSE, CLANTON (1896)

Architect: W. S. Hull; Builder: J. H. Duke

When its frame 1872 courthouse had outlived its usefulness, Chilton County replaced it with a more substantial brick building with contrasting white stone trim, on a coursed rubble foundation. In appearance it might be mistaken for any public school building of the period, were it not for its imposing bell tower and the small spires that decorate the roof. The irregular placement of windows on the right side of the façade reveals that a staircase giving access to the second floor was placed here. Judging from the many window openings for that second floor, a courtroom occupied most of the space.

Notwithstanding its masonry construction, the interior of the Chilton County courthouse burned in 1918. But the foresight of the county in providing a fireproof records storage vault saved it from the fate of the many Alabama counties whose courthouses and county records have been destroyed by fire. Chilton County replaced the partially burned 1896 courthouse with a fashionable neoclassical one in 1919.

CHILTON COUNTY COURTHOUSE, CLANTON (1919)

Architect: Frank Lockwood; Builder: F. M. Dobson

Some uncertainty attaches to the construction of the Chilton County courthouse of 1919. After the previous courthouse burned in 1918, a grand jury charged to investigate the disaster did not report that arson was involved. The interior was the principal casualty, for photographs show that the walls still stood after the fire. Minutes of the County Commissioners record bids for replacing the courthouse. All specify an amount for "rebuilding" it. The winning bid, from F. M. Dobson, reads, "I will rebuild your old Court House according to plans and specifications as prepared and furnished by Mr. Frank Lockwood, architect, of Montgomery, Alab., including the front addition as shown thereon for the lump sum of $28,744.00 . . ." Views of the building, as shown above, suggest then the possibility that the rear section is the rebuilt courthouse of 1896 and the front section is new construction, in a Lockwood neoclassical mode with grand tetrastyle Ionic portico sheltering an elaborate front door surround with broken arched pediment supported by brackets. Another indication of the rebuilding of the rear portion may be that the first-floor window tops do not match those of the front portion of the building. Sanborn Fire Insurance Co. maps for 1917 and 1928 show similar footprints for the Chilton County courthouses of 1872 and 1896 except that the 1928 map shows the left side of the front section extending almost to the street, while the 1917 map does not.

Replacing the old courthouse threatened the county's financial future to such an extent that the Board of Supervisors canceled home and farm demonstration and road maintenance programs at the same meeting in which they accepted Lockwood's plans and hired contractor Dobson. For more than forty years Chilton County conducted its official business in this building. It was razed upon the completion of a new courthouse on a different site.

Choctaw Historical Society

CHOCTAW COUNTY COURTHOUSE, BUTLER (1906)

Architect: William S. Hull, Mr. Payne;
Builder: Hugger Brothers, George Tillmon, Jim Bush

Later nineteenth - and early twentieth-century courthouse design included several features to enhance the provision of the public services county organization provided. A bell tower to signal alarm, celebration, or necessary attendance was one usual device; another was the clock atop the building, often a public necessity before watches were common. But patrons had to find the courthouses before they could use its services. Central location was an obvious advantage, often on or adjacent to a central public square, and often on a street with a giveaway name like Court Street or Government Street. Some buildings announced just by their architecture that they were courthouses, not schools or churches or banks. One of these is the ochre brick Choctaw County courthouse in Butler that the Hugger Brothers constructed from William S. Hull's plans. No dome or bell or clock tower is needed to announce that this is a courthouse, though its location did. The portico tells much of this building's story by drawing upon a traditional courthouse vocabulary—classical pedimentation above an arcaded first-floor entrance. Its identity is enhanced by its masonry, by multiple public entrances, by the impression of solidity conveyed in the underlying block, even by the ornamentation of the structures of uncertain purposes that pierce the roof. Several modern-era additions to the Choctaw County courthouse have done little to improve its original appearance (cf. Washington County courthouse of 1908).

Clarke County Historical Museum

CLARKE COUNTY COURTHOUSE, GROVE HILL (1837, 1877)

Architect: Unrecorded; Builder: Unrecorded

As early frame courthouses in Alabama go, Clarke County's seems quite respectable. The skimpy shed roof over the left entrance suggests it was a service entrance of some kind, perhaps even admitting a judge to a small chamber behind his bench in a courtroom entered primarily from the sheltered door to the right. Peeking from behind the courthouse is a jail, seemingly of brick, and having at least one flue that could have afforded heat to inmates. No such flue is apparent in the courthouse image; perhaps courts were not held during infrequent bitter cold.

In the gable end of the building, above the left entrance one can make out a window. Considering how far the weatherboarded wall extends above the first-floor window tops, some sort of usable space may have existed under the roof, probably not a gallery above the courtroom, but at least storage space. Along with many of its sister counties, Clarke did not remain content with this old but useful frame courthouse, replacing it in 1899 with an "up-to-date" brick building.

Clarke County Historical Museum

CLARKE COUNTY COURTHOUSE, GROVE HILL (1899)

Architect: Frank B. Hull; Builder: William S. Hull & Samuel Ewing

Clarke Countians should not have been surprised by the appearance of their new courthouse, for, had they been looking, they might have seen it all before. Though not an exact replica, it is in many respects a sibling of the Chilton County courthouse built in Clanton in 1896, which is no surprise because the Mississippian William Hull was a parent to both. The detailed description of the completed courthouse published in the *Clarke County Democrat* reveals how up-to-date the gray brick building was. Even allowing for the boosterish tone in which local newspapers invariably bragged about new courthouses, the description testifies to a well thought out plan, quality materials, and competent construction skills, producing an architectural result more often found in an urban setting than in the public buildings of rural Alabama counties.

CLAY COUNTY COURTHOUSE, ASHLAND (1876)

Architect: Unrecorded; Builder: Unrecorded

Courthouses using a double exterior staircase (in several variations) to enter second-floor courtrooms are sometimes referred to as "open-arms" courthouses. The form was often used in courthouse buildings for counties to which early or large portions of new settlers emigrated from South Carolina, where the style was popular. Alabamians have used it for such elegant courthouses as those in Lowndes and Butler counties and for plainer ones in Lee and this one in Clay County. The photograph above, as indistinct as it is, tells us almost all we wish to know about the building. With a number of windows extending along each side, both up and down, the first floor, entered under the staircase, would be used for county offices with access from the hallway running through its center. A rear door may have opened at the far end of the hall. Upstairs, the courtroom was entered at the rear, with judge's bench facing this doorway, probably the only entrance/exit to and from the floor. Behind the judge's bench may have been a judge's chamber and/or jury room(s); judging the size of the building from what we see here, it would be as likely that one or both of these amenities were omitted. The history of many counties repeats itself here in accounting for the building. The original log courthouse and all the county records in it burned. In the greater security of this red brick structure, the county carried on for the next thirty years.

CLAY COUNTY COURTHOUSE, ASHLAND (1906)

Architect: Charles W. Carlton; Builder: Harper & Barnes

Whether architect Charles Carlton was at the top of his game in designing this courthouse is a matter of debate, but at least his building stands literally higher than any other Alabama courthouse. Anniston's Charles Carlton, once an associate of R. H. Hunt, produced for Clay County a building that may not have been considered brilliant, but it had enough bells-and-whistles to please the local citizens, both county officialdom and ordinary taxpayers. Perhaps influenced by J. W. Golucke's courthouse designs, Carlton included here a rusticated ground floor with arcaded entrance; *piano nobile* behind recessed upper level porches with classical columns and pediments, pitched roof hidden behind a decorated parapet wall, minor corner domes at the roofline, and, presiding over it all, a domed central tower composed of a tall drum pierced by narrow windows and "bullseye" windows above them; finally, four clock faces at the bottom of the dome and a tall lantern at its top, finished off by a statue of Justice with Scales. From this courthouse, Clay County native, former U.S. Senator and Supreme Court Justice Hugo L. Black began his legal career.

CLEBURNE COUNTY COURTHOUSE, EDWARDSVILLE (C. 1869–70)

Architect: Unrecorded; Builder: Unrecorded

Before moving the county seat to Heflin, the Cleburne County courthouse was located in Edwardsville and, fortunately, was well documented in the Historic American Buildings Survey. This large brick building, 60' x 40', is there described in these terms: "hipped roof, brick water table and belt course, segmental arched masonry openings with projecting voussoirs."

But HABS, rather sadly, added, "original plan much altered for present use as school." The unbalanced arrangement of bays showing in this photograph might suggest that each floor of this façade originally had more openings, but the arrangement of flues piercing the roof makes this unlikely. In fact, it was the arrangement of first-floor offices that dictated the window spacing.

The lower door showing in the photographs opened onto a broad corridor running through the building to a matching door on the other side. This corridor is the crossing of a T made by another corridor running through the center of the building to the right and another door on the shorter side of the courthouse. The second floor, as usual, was given over to courtroom and adjoining chambers for judges and juries.

Curiously, the HABS reconstruction of the courthouse floor plans shows no stair to the upper floor. However, a door opening into the courtroom from the shorter side of the building (to the right, above), and the symmetrical arrangement of doors and windows in this side of the building, leads to the conclusion that this was the principal public entrance to the courthouse and that an exterior (and probably double) staircase of some kind was the principal (and only) entrance into the second-floor courtroom.

Birmingham Public Library

CLEBURNE COUNTY COURTHOUSE, HEFLIN (1907)

Architect: Charles W. Carlton; Builder: F. B. Hull Construction Co.

The same Charles W. Carlton who designed the Clay County courthouse next door, designed this one for Cleburne County at Heflin a year later. Though individual features vary, the basic mass and style of the two buildings is the same and the general impression given by both is similar. Just as in Clay County, the architect's composition relies on a rusticated ground floor with arcaded entrance, *piano nobile*, and neoclassical portico (but here engaged rather than recessed. The building is somewhat smaller than its neighbor and lacks the monumental side entrances. The scale of the square clock-and-bell tower is well suited to the size of the building, as are other more modest features of the design, such as the simple unadorned semi-circular window heads, and the stepped rooflines. The wings added to the building in 1938 considerably diminished its modesty. Fortunately, they are in an appropriate style to complement to the original building although they give a horizontal effect to the courthouse rather than its original vertical appearance.

The reliable and experienced Frank Hull was the contractor for Heflin's Cleburne County courthouse. His Mississippi-based construction company seems to have bid on every Alabama courthouse project announced while the company was in business, and he bid successfully on many. The Hull Brothers were in the vanguard of a small but growing number of regional construction companies that through economies of scale and access to improving transportation and communications facilities could successfully bid against local contractors, producing more buildings in shorter times at lower costs.

Alabama Department of Archives and History

COFFEE COUNTY COURTHOUSE, ELBA (1882, 1899)

Architect: and Builder: M. M. Tye

Two photographs (of which this is one) identified as the Coffee County courthouse at Elba have been filed at the Alabama Department of Archives and History for a number of years. When one was used in a public display recently, a visitor objected that the building was the Coffee County High School at Enterprise rather than the courthouse. Characteristics of the building are sufficient to make a case for either use.

It is known that M. M. Tye expanded his Coffee County courthouse in 1899 with a wing to the rear, thus preserving the symmetry of the front of the building. Some details of the building are obscured in this photograph, leaving largely to our imagination the exact configuration of the roof. For instance, how the twin pyramidal roofs that cover the outer sections of the building might be joined behind the central tower is puzzling. The tower itself is a puzzle, for there are no clock faces evident on it. Ribbon windows on the front of the building seem to be sets of triple sash to the left and right of the tower section, making difficult any assumption about a presumed second-floor courtroom. Even so, what we can see in this view looks quite up to Tye's standard of building substantial structures with good proportions and enough style to satisfy the tastes of even fussy county commissioners.

Despite the 1899 expansion of the courthouse, it still proved inadequate for the rapidly expanding Coffee County population. County authorities razed the building just three years later to build a larger one, itself to be later expanded even further.

Author's collection

COFFEE COUNTY COURTHOUSE, ELBA (1903)

Architect: Andrew J. Bryan; Builder: M. T. Lewman & Co.

Andrew Bryan was an ambitious, hardworking, sometimes quirky, and often disappointed architect trying to make his way in the increasingly competitive business of professional architecture in the American South between about 1880 and 1920. Bryan moved his practice from Atlanta to Jackson, Mississippi, to New Orleans, and finally to Louisville, in search of work and reputation. The Coffee County courthouse at Elba was the earliest of Bryan's five Alabama courthouses. If the design was intended to be Romanesque, as some have described it, it was only a modest success. But for the tower and the conical turret caps, it might be taken for a factory building, an impression deepened by the absence of a cornice. This Coffee County courthouse has survived, albeit with ungainly wings added. It has often been photographed standing in floodwaters when the nearby Pea River overflowed its banks.

COLBERT COUNTY COURTHOUSE, TUSCUMBIA (1882)

Architect: Edward Laurent; Builder: William Dowling

For its first permanent courthouse, Colbert County erected a brick building including what one might identify as Second Empire features, the convex mansard roofs that flank the central block of the building. Into these roofs, the architect set decorated round windows. Stone trimmings in a light shade to contrast with dark brick walls were used for belt courses, semi-circular arches above second floor and tower windows and for bracketed lintels over segmentally arched ground-floor windows. The complex impression the building gives viewers is due principally to the massive corner tower with its louvered belfry and tall convex mansard roof ornamented by large round clock faces. The raised pedimented central pavilion was the likely location of a second-floor courtroom.

Though not literally on the Tennessee border, Colbert County could claim as many connections with that state as with Alabama. Little surprise then that both the architect and the builder for its 1882 courthouse were Tennesseans, both coming to Tuscumbia as established professionals. Edward Laurent, the architect for the Colbert courthouse, was an important contributor to the architectural scene in Nashville, both as architect and builder. He would later (1897) serve as contractor, though not architect, for Nashville's Parthenon. The Irish immigrant William Dowling was known as the builder of the Hamilton County courthouse in Chattanooga, and the auditorium for the university of that city (now University of Tennessee at Chattanooga).

Author's collection

COLBERT COUNTY COURTHOUSE, TUSCUMBIA (1909)

Architect: Bearden & Forman, C. L. Peckinpaugh; Builder: Holsford & Graham

While Colbert County has a fair claim to having the most attractive Alabama courthouse, the details of how it achieved this result are still not entirely clear. In particular, we do not know today just what was the relationship between Bearden & Forman, the Chattanooga architectural firm, and C. L. Peckinpaugh, from nearby Sheffield. While news reports refer to them as "associate architects," that may mean that Peckinpaugh was the supervising architect, Bearden & Forman contributing the general design work.

When the courthouse of 1882 was gutted by fire in May of 1908, the county moved quickly to overcome the disaster. Over the course of the next year, Colbert officials settled a problematic insurance claim, hired another Tennessee architect, successfully organized and won a bond referendum, and oversaw completion of the courthouse rebuilding, this time hiring a local contracting firm, Holsford & Graham of neighboring Florence, rather than another Tennessee builder.

The result was a true rebuilding, for despite the 1908 fire, the walls of the old building were still standing and were usable. Comparing the available fire insurance maps before and after the fire (i.e., Sanborn maps of 1905 and 1910) clearly shows the newer building is the older one revised and added to. (Notwithstanding the fire in 1908, the Sanborn map for 1910 notes, "Fire Proof const. except Roof.) The corner tower of 1882 is gone; an elaborate domed clock tower is centered on the 1909 roof. The neoclassical impression given by the generous porticoes and standard details of the style is not even threatened by the odd serrated lower edge of the belt course running between the building's pilasters.

Evergreen-Conecuh Public Library

CONECUH COUNTY COURTHOUSE, EVERGREEN (1883)

Architect: Unrecorded; Builder: Unrecorded

This somewhat ungainly structure was the second Conecuh County courthouse built in Evergreen, the third or fourth in the county, but the first of brick. Perhaps attempting to give a civic presence to the very plain and basic box containing first-floor offices and second-floor courtroom, the builders added the heavy colonnade of square pillars, topped by a "cornice of unimaginative design" that conceals a roof of very shallow pitch, apparently drained by such downfalls as can be seen attached to the side wall near the front of the building. The only relief to the stern appearance of the building is offered by the balusters of the stair railing that appear to be either turned or sawed in some two dimensional pattern. Just as in many of the Alabama courthouses of this period, the double outside staircases suggest the lingering influence of Carolina courthouse designs carried west with migrating families.

Author's collection

CONECUH COUNTY COURTHOUSE, EVERGREEN (1901)

Architect: Frank Lockwood and B. B. Smith; Builder: William A. Andrews

Architect Frank Lockwood used the same Romanesque Revival vocabulary for his later Baldwin County courthouse that made the Conecuh County courthouse such a treasure in the town of Evergreen. Neo-Romanesque, one of the many revival styles of the late Victorian period, appeared in Lockwood's work here in the arched entrance, steep hipped roof, turrets, and rounded apse-like projections at the sides. This is a style for public buildings. Part of Lockwood's success here was that, although in an ensemble one might think this was an academic building, standing prominently in a townscape it could only be a courthouse.

In plan, the building was almost symmetrical, roughly a T-shape with fat arms and leg. The tower reached 75' skyward. Although lit by electricity, the heating equipment was "stoves and grates" and, judging by the number of flues pictured here, there would not have been many of those.

In a controversial move, the county authorities retained the modernist architect Martin Lide to design a new front to this building in the 1950s. The 1899 Conecuh County courthouse fell to the wrecker's ball in 2005, despite vigorous and sustained opposition within the county and from preservationists over the state, and despite legal challenges. Sadly neglected and mistreated over years, it was "beyond feasible to repair," according to county authorities.

Coosa County Historical Society

COOSA COUNTY COURTHOUSE, ROCKFORD (1858)

Architect: William Jenkins (1858); E. J. Ostling (1904);
Builder: Henry Etter and E. H. Grady (1858); F. M. Dobson (1904)

The Coosa County courthouse has weathered fire and periodic remodeling so that the building that still stands in Rockford bears only a passing resemblance to its original appearance. However, both as originally built in 1858 and as remodeled in 1902 as shown in this photograph, its architectural character is unique among Alabama's courthouse. Some suppose that the design pictured in this photograph falls in the Second Empire category, though no characteristic mansard roof covered the building, nor did any of the minor features of the style support identifying it as Second Empire. It is difficult to know whether the central portion of the façade is a true loggia or whether the lower floor contains stairs to the second floor entrance in a recessed portico (as it is today). In any case the central portion of the façade perhaps retains elements of the original building with (at least) columns and a pediment perhaps with acroterium, but otherwise the façade is part of the 1902 renovation.

The curiously bell-shaped domes upon octagonal bases that cover the pavilions flanking the "portico" do not appear functional at all—that is, no clock, no bell. In subsequent remodeling of the building they were removed. The eaves project from the roofline unusually far and the brackets under them are spaced more widely than one expects. Still, the bracketed cornice ties the various parts of the building together as it runs completely around the structure.

The original construction is sometimes attributed to Patrick Coniff, who later built the 1861 Tallapoosa County courthouse. Coosa County records, however, show that while Coniff bid for the contract and worked on the building, Etter and Grady were the contractors of record. Interestingly, some of the payments to Grady were made to "A. E. [sic] Grady and S. E. Grady, Contractors of Court House." S. E. Grady was Sarah E., E. H. Grady's wife!

NGTON COUNTY COURT HOUSE,
ANDALUSIA, ALA.

935a

Keith Vincent, *CourthouseHistory*

COVINGTON COUNTY COURTHOUSE, ANDALUSIA (1897)

Architect: Walter Chamberlin; Builder: B. C. Williams

Walter Chamberlin, designer of the Covington County courthouse, had begun his practice in Knoxville and later moved it to Birmingham. He was one of a group of New South architects who regularly faced each other in courthouse design competitions across most of the southeastern states, a group that included A. J. Bryan, J. W. Golucke, E. C. Hosford, Frank Milburn, and P. H. Weathers.

The courthouse that Chamberlin designed for Covington County once stood in the middle of Andalusia's courthouse square, the same location of an earlier wooden courthouse that an arsonist may have burned. The two-story brick building shows Chamberlin's talent before he produced a number of courthouses that bear a "characteristic" Chamberlin signature in the unusual configuration of their towers (cf. Crenshaw, *infra*). But here the arrangement of separate towers for clock and for bell seems to arise naturally from the advanced bays on which they sit. The rusticated brickwork of the bays and entry between them provide a relieving contrast to the plain brick surfaces on either side.

The building stood on the square while the next, grandiose Covington County courthouse was under construction. The debate that arose about the desirability of a new building, not about the inadequacies of the old, ended finally in the triumph of Covington County officials' hope for what the county might become over many citizens' satisfaction with what it was.

COVINGTON COUNTY COURTHOUSE, ANDALUSIA (1916)

Architect: Frank Lockwood and Frederick Ausfeld; Builder: Little-Cleckler Construction

If ever a building had a traumatic gestation, it was the Covington County courthouse, finally born in 1916. The conception took place in 1914; before the actual birth, the county authorities (in the form of the Board of Revenue of Covington County) had run through two and perhaps three architects (H. L. Lewman, W. L. Stevens, Frank Lockwood-Frederick Ausfeld) and two contractors (Falls City Construction Company, Little-Cleckler Construction Company), defended a suit over a disputed county election, settled outstanding claims brought against it by one disappointed contractor, and finally depended on the Alabama Supreme Court to quash an injunction against building a new courthouse at all (*Board of Revenue of Covington County v. Merrill*, 193 Ala. 521, 1915).

Undeterred by any of this, the county fathers barged ahead with plans from Montgomery architects Frank Lockwood and Frederick Ausfeld to raise a building they deemed more suitable than Chamberlin's 1897 courthouse to the ambitions of south Alabama and of Andalusia in particular. This granite building overlooks the courthouse square rather than standing upon it. Indeed, it extends the entire length of one side of that square to which it offers a grand classical hexastyle portico with correct Corinthian detailing. On both sides of the portico, pilasters separate the three-bay compositions of the wings. The arrangement is enhanced by varying roof levels; an attic feature behind the portico pediment raises the central portion of the roof above the height of the wings. In the event, the quality of the building did little to mollify opponents. In time, public opinion moved through resignation to admiration today.

Crenshaw County Courthouse
Luverne, Ala.

Author's collection

CRENSHAW COUNTY COURTHOUSE, LUVERNE (1889)

Architect: Walter Chamberlin; Builder: Arnold Hugger & Co.

Not every courthouse that Walter Chamberlin designed looked like the one in Crenshaw County. But many did. With only a little searching, one could find Crenshaw look-alikes as nearby as Selma, and as far away as Pulaski, Virginia. Recognition depends on only a few elements—the shape of the clock tower set above an open belfry, square corner rooms projecting outward from the main block and fitted with pyramidal roofs, and main doorway set between advanced blocks rising above the line of the eaves and capped with imaginative finials. Counties that built these courthouses cannot have been unaware that their buildings were just variations of plans adopted by other counties. Perhaps the choice was driven by thriftiness, although we have no record showing that Chamberlin offered a cut rate for his cookie-cutter courthouses.

Even though the format that Chamberlin used here apparently had a widespread aesthetic appeal, it ultimately fell to the need for greater spaces. In planning the altogether undistinguished building that replaced this one in 1950, county officials dismissed the possibility of an addition to the 1899 structure. Considering the disaster of the addition placed onto Frank Lockwood's Conecuh County courthouse, addition might have been a risky choice, but other choices might have preserved this very serviceable reminder of a hopeful time in the county's history.

Cullman County Courthouse, Cullman (1879)

Architect: Unrecorded; Builder: Nelson

Despite the essentially German heritage of the founders and settlers in the Cullman area, there is nothing especially Teutonic about this courthouse, built shortly after voters chose the town of Cullman to be the seat of Cullman County. And that may have been just the point; cultural assimilation has seemed a rational strategy for many immigrant groups. In plan, the building was quite simple—a square with each side divided into thirds. On the front side the middle third was recessed, the main entrance on the first floor, a balcony on the second, and a gable in the roof. On each of the other three sides, the middle third projected. (Later fire insurance maps, however, show all four sides with the same projecting third.) The light color of the coursed rubble foundation contrasted attractively with the deep red of the brick walls. Their corner pilasters were topped with a busy cornice below the eaves of the hipped roof. What draws the eye from this dignified composition is, however, the tower centered on the roof. No clock or bell is evident in old photographs of the building, so its purpose may only have been to introduce light into the center of the building.

Court House, Cullman, Ala.

Author's collection

CULLMAN COUNTY COURTHOUSE, CULLMAN (1912)

Architect: William A. Schlosser; Builder: F. M. Dobson

Cullman County authorities announced in 1905 that they had hired Jackson, Mississippi's reliable William S. Hull to design an extension to the 1879 courthouse and a new jail building. Nothing came of the intention, but the county's hand was forced when the old courthouse was seriously damaged by fire. The county commissioners then decided to repair the damage and proceed with an extension of the building. Finally, that plan, too, was discarded and Cullman County moved ahead to build a new—and very grand—courthouse, this one designed by W. A. Schlosser, a local Cullman architect. F. M. Dobson of Jasper submitted the winning bid of $54,000 to become the building's contractor.

Schlosser's design was grand neoclassical stuff, and it was pretty well stuffed with nearly every bell-and-whistle in the neoclassical catalog. Its red brick barely peeked through the white curtain of porticoes with monumental Scamozzi Ionic columns, quoins at corners and pilasters matching them, windows accented with stone lintels (round arched above, square-head below), cornice and modillions. Riding over this ensemble was a square tower of four short windowed sides and a roof of four curved panels rising to a rather squat finial. Each of the four roof panels held a clock face.

DALE COUNTY COURTHOUSE, OZARK (1885)

Architect and Builder: M. M. Tye

Though Milton M. Tye was a local builder, operating from Ozark as M. M. Tye and Son, his work can also be found in adjoining areas of Florida and Georgia. So far as is now known, Tye built only to his own designs. The courthouse he planned and built for his home county, Dale, was quite plain; only the double outside stair to the second-floor columned portico (barely visible in this image) adorned it at all. Doubtless this feature shows that the second floor was reserved for courtroom and spaces for jury and judge, with apartments for county offices on the ground floor. But Tye could produce high-style buildings as well as plain ones; see, for example, his courthouses for Bullock, Coffee, and Geneva counties in Alabama and Walton County in Florida.

While Tye fit comfortably into the category of local builder, the day of local self-taught designers—for Tye was not professionally trained—was waning with the nineteenth century. The competition in public building design included more and more professionally trained architects—the Bryans and Chamberlins and Goluckes, etc.—who ambitiously exhibited their talents on a much larger stage, the whole southeastern U.S. Tye as a contractor was equally as qualified as any against whom he competed for contracts, but either a more modest ambition or some limitation in organizational skills confined his contributions in building to a rather small part of the Southeast.

Court House Square on a busy day, Ozark, Ala.

DALE COUNTY COURTHOUSE, OZARK (1902)

Architect: Andrew J. Bryan; Builder: M. T. Lewman & Co.

The Dale County courthouse, raised in 1902, stood on the central square of Ozark until 1968 when it was taken down despite energetic community efforts to save it. Many of the photographs of the building circulating today picture it as white, but for its first fifty years, the rich red brick was unpainted. Unlike its smaller, simple and modest predecessor, this building was large, complicated, and grandiose. The ground floor consisted of a maze of suites with inner and outer offices, opening off a central hall running from front entrance to rear. The style, according to a report in an Ozark newspaper, "reflected the architecture of the period with its Gothic turrets, arches, [and] peaks." While one might debate its "Gothic" character, it certainly is true that this is the architecture of the period.

Dale County hired a prolific designer-builder team for this project. Both Bryan and the Lewman company were independent operators at this time, though later they entered into a formal partnership. They were the same pair that built many courthouses over the southeast, including the well-known and admired Monroe County courthouse in Monroeville, Alabama. The assemblage of architectural elements around the entrance to this building is one that Bryan used in several other courthouses, for example, the nearby Coffee County courthouse in Elba (*supra*) or the Pointe Coupee Parish Courthouse in New Roads, Louisiana.

DALLAS COUNTY COURTHOUSE, CAHAWBA (1834)

Architect and Builder: Unrecorded (perhaps Benjamin H. Cameron)

Following the history of Dallas County courthouses when the county seat was still at Cahawba taxes the ingenuity of any historian. The county had inherited the former Alabama statehouse when the state capital was moved to Tuscaloosa. The old capitol, that became the Dallas County courthouse, was too damaged by flooding to be used by the county. Its bricks, however, were salvaged and used to construct the building pictured here. The resemblance between this building and the Chambers County courthouse (*q.v.*) is so close that attributing it to the prolific and peripatetic builder from Troup County, Georgia, Benjamin Cameron, seems warranted. Not surprisingly, little history remains of this building, for the county seat was moved to Selma by virtue of a referendum in 1866, from which point Cahawba was virtually abandoned and its buildings, including this one, gradually disappeared from a variety of causes.

This photograph shows the building in a state of deterioration, but placement of the rounded-transom doorways suggests that the ground office floor was divided by crossing hallways and that the second floor courtroom was reached by an interior stair, for considering the second floor window arrangement, there would have been none outside of the building. That the gable ends were rendered as pediments shows that some architectural pretensions operated in the project, and the double circular, or perhaps oval, openings (or perhaps just decorations) underline that possibility.

Alabama Department of Archives and History

DALLAS COUNTY COURTHOUSE, SELMA (1902)

Architect: Walter Chamberlin; Builder: John W. Hood & Buchell

More elaborate than the Crenshaw County courthouse (*q.v.*), the building that Walter Chamberlin designed for Dallas County as the first purpose-built courthouse in Selma, is nonetheless instantly recognizable as a Chamberlin product by anyone familiar with his work. The projecting corner rooms with sharply peaked pyramidal roofs, the blocks that flank entrances to the building and rise above the eave lines, and above all the composition of the soaring tower—open boxy bell chamber below, and diminishing elements above including a roof composed of steep, curving panels, and a pinnacle to top off the whole composition. Romanesque? Well, perhaps; but not a very conventional Romanesque.

Whether from some flaw in the design or some negligence by the builder, John Hood of Montgomery, or for some other reason, in 1957 the tower fell into the center of the building, but left undamaged an annex that was incorporated into a new building that the county government occupied in 1960.

Birmingham Public Library

DeKalb County Courthouse, Lebanon (1842)

Architect: Unrecorded; Builder: Unrecorded

The photograph above shows the building that had been the DeKalb County courthouse, without its later alterations. About 1890 (below), with an elaborate gallery, the upper floor was a family residence and the lower a commercial space. In the 1960s the again-renovated building was rented to the public for weddings and other social events.

To secure the county seat for Lebanon, two local families, the Fraziers and the Dobbses, donated the land for the building and may have had some part in constructing it. Specula-

University of Alabama

tion about the designer/ builder has also included Vance Larmore, a prominent citizen and architect/builder in DeKalb County, who is especially remembered as a builder of homes. Tragically, Larmore died in 1886 when his neck was broken by a falling tree.

DeKalb County Courthouse, Fort Payne (1876)

Architect: Unrecorded; Builder: John N. B. Faulkner & Dilly Towers

For the convenient conduct of county business, Lebanon proved to be no match for its growing neighbors. In a contest for location of the county seat in 1890, Lebanon was not even a candidate. Winner by a slim margin was Fort Payne which had everything a county seat needed—population, central location, and, above all, the railroad. What it did not have when it won the prize was a courthouse. Perhaps its haste to build one explains this quite plain courthouse design, a tribute to expediency and thrift, perhaps, but hardly to civic pride or ambition. The builders are memorable not for producing a memorable building but for their unforgettable names—"John *Napoleon Bonaparte* Faulkner" and "*Dilly* Towers." Both were masons by trade; apparently Faulkner was the principal builder, for county histories invariably say he was "assisted by an experienced bricklayer named Dilly Towers."

The plan of the building may be read in part from its appearance in the view above. On the first floor, a hallway bisects the building from the front door to another at the rear. There is no evidence of a crossing hallway from side to side, but it is likely that such a passage divided the first floor into four offices without exterior side doors. A stair led to the upper floor courtroom from which speakers could appear through the centered doorway onto a small platform to address public gatherings outside the building.

Author's Collection

COURT HOUSE FORT PAYNE ALA.

DeKalb County Courthouse, Fort Payne (1892)

Architect: Chamberlin & Burford; Builder: Pearce & Morgan

Before Walter Chamberlin hit on the style that attracted Crenshaw and Dallas counties, he produced more conventional courthouse designs such as this one in Fort Payne for DeKalb County. The sober and straightforward building was composed of basically the same masses that architect B. B. Smith assembled with more flair for his neoclassical 1903 Butler County courthouse (*q.v.*). The style is roughly neo-Romanesque for the semi-circular door and window surrounds and the steeply pitched roofs on the corner towers and central soaring bell tower. Even though no clock was in place when the building was first occupied, space was thoughtfully provided for one and, indeed, a large clock face eventually was installed below the belfry.

The purpose of the one-story apse on the right side is not clear. In the Butler courthouse, matching two-story apses project from both sides and are a design feature of the second-floor courtroom. But in Fort Payne, the first-floor apse is simply part of one office, as is revealed by the presence of a records vault next to the space. The courtroom is, as usual, a second-floor feature, here reached by twin interior staircases.

John Enslen

ELMORE COUNTY COURTHOUSE, WETUMPKA (1885)

Architect: Unrecorded; Builder: Arthur Marshall

As in a number of other Alabama counties, Elmore's courthouse featured a double outside stair to reach the second-floor courtroom. And like many of those, in its early years Elmore had a strong connection to South Carolina, where this feature of courthouse was common. Even though General Elmore, for whom the county is named, was born in Virginia, he came to prominence in South Carolina where he had served in the state legislature, and from where he entered military service during the American Revolutionary War. His descendants were the prominent settlers of what became Elmore County in 1866. Although in some photographs the courthouse appears to be crowded within the city blocks, in fact, it was surrounded by generous grounds and by the Coosa River on one side. The somewhat quirky building has a semicircular gable over the center bay, presumably to mirror the semicircular arches of the doors on both floors and the double arches over the elongated double windows on the second (courtroom) floor. These, along with the double brackets under the eaves, give the building a slight Italianate flavor. A common drawback in this type of design is that the double outside stair to the second floor often crosses in front of the first-floor windows, as is the case here (and see Wilcox County courthouse similarly), although using cast iron minimizes the blockage of light into the front offices.

This building was in use through the construction beside it of the next Elmore County courthouse, the handsome classical building that still stands. Some of the few photographs of the 1885 courthouse are available because it can be seen in the background of construction images of its successor and through the process of its demolition.

Jefferson Davis Community College

Escambia County Courthouse, Brewton (1885)

Architect: Rudolph Benz; Builder: Charles Schneider

Some confusion attends identifying the architect of the 1885 Escambia County courthouse because the design has been attributed to Rudolph Bundley or Bundye. However, a comparison of the building with that of Baldwin County in Daphne *(q.v.)* makes clear that Rudolph Benz, the Mobile architect, was the designer of this square building in Brewton with fancifully decorated gables on all sides.

After a number of renovations and conversions, the building still stands in Brewton under the name "Leigh Place."

Author's collection

ESCAMBIA COUNTY COURTHOUSE, BREWTON (1902)

Architect: Frank Lockwood and B. B. Smith; Builder: F. M. Dobson

The courthouses for Baldwin, Butler, Conecuh, and Escambia counties, all designed by Frank Lockwood (with B. B. Smith in the cases of Baldwin and Escambia), and all built by F. M. Dobson, are "variations on a theme." Though their principal facades seemed distinctively different, their footprints were nearly identical. The "theme" is not only the neo-Romanesque style of the buildings (although with occasional unusual embellishments to that style), but more significantly the way that Lockwood assembled their volumes. The principal tower in Escambia rises from a triple arched loggia, richly ornamented with bas-relief terra cotta. Behind the several towers and semicircular openings of the arcade, the principal mass of the building is a rectangular block (sometimes with stubby projections on both of the shorter sides). Behind that is another rectangular block, almost as deep but not as wide. Projecting octagonal extensions of the far corners of this rear block complete the basic plan. Rather than simply decorating a more straightforward underlying box, Lockwood matched the complications of the decorations with an equally complicated plan, *de rigueur*, apparently, for the time and for his clients.

Detail from map at Library of Congress

Etowah County Courthouse, Gadsden (1870)

Architect: Unrecorded; Builder: R. B. Kyle & W. P. Hollingsworth

No photographs of the first Etowah County courthouse are known, but it is included on an 1887 panoramic map of Gadsden, as shown in the detail above from the drawing. The "A" on the roof of the building is keyed to the legend identifying the most important buildings in the town. That the courthouse would stand first on that list, as well as its central geographic position in the town, certainly indicates its importance as the center of the life in the community.

So far as one can judge, the building is not simply an intruder among more sophisticated neighbors. Facing on Gadsden's Broad Street, the courthouse offered to the public's view a tetrastyle portico under which, we are told, a small balcony permitted addressing assembled citizens below. The drawing also includes some sort of embellishment at the window heads and a generous entablature below the roof line. The image is not clear enough to establish whether the rear of the roof is pedimented or hipped. The belfry on the roof , though not strictly correct stylistically, would have been thought a civic necessity to provide warnings of impending dangers, to call the community together for important civic duties, and to add celebratory notes to momentous events.

Court House, Gadsden, Ala.—12

ETOWAH COUNTY COURTHOUSE, GADSDEN (1891)

Architect: John A. Scott; Builder: T. B. Gwin, M. L. Hicks & M. E. Lane

This large and complicated building served Etowah County for sixty years during which its appearance had been altered by reconfiguring the clock tower roof, painting the brick, and several times reconstructing the stairs to the building entrance. Details of the construction recorded on fire insurance maps show that the contractors, Gwin, Hicks & Lane (who ran the Gadsden Planing Mills and must have subcontracted extensively) made the building to last. "All floors 1, 2, 3 are laid on 4" of cement with IR [iron] ceiling supporting that. We also find, "2 fl. French Roof," that is, "mansard roof," difficult to make out behind the various structures that interrupt it. Before a large addition was added to the rear of this building, eight offices opened from the central corridor of the first floor which was entered from the recessed loggia facing the street. And, as usual, the second floor was devoted to the courtroom and auxiliary judicial spaces.

Building a new courthouse has often been contentious in Alabama counties, but in Etowah county in the 1940s the issue was joined not over irregularities in the authority of the county to build a new courthouse but whether it was within its right to sell the site of the one, pictured here, and build anew on another site. The Alabama Supreme Court decided that it was. (*Board of Revenue of Etowah County, et al. v. Hutchins*, 250 Ala. 173.)

Glenn Holliman

FAYETTE COUNTY COURTHOUSE, FAYETTE (1892)

Architect: E. J. Ostling & Son; Builder: Unrecorded

Even though the Fayette County courthouse of 1858 stood until the 1890s, no photographs are available to show us what it was like. After the great fire that nearly leveled the growing town of Fayette in the early spring of 1911, an indistinct photograph is almost all that remains to tell us much about the courthouse that E. J. Ostling produced for Fayette County. Ostling designed courthouses and jails from offices in Montgomery and Tuscaloosa before moving on to Indianapolis. The somewhat military appearance of the crenellated entrance suggests a Gothic style; however, the treatments of roofs, upper-story window heads, pilastered corners of the building, and horseshoe entrance would suggest more a Romanesque mode.

Fayette Times Record

FAYETTE COUNTY COURTHOUSE, FAYETTE (1912)

Architect: H. E. Ostling; Builder: Little-Cleckler Construction Co.

If pinning down the style of its 1892 courthouse is problematic, no such difficulty attends Fayette County's 1912 courthouse; it is emphatically neoclassical (as seen here behind the crowd gathered for its dedication)—from its pedimented tetrastyle porticoes with colossal ionic columns to the lantern sitting atop a hemispheric dome atop a square windowed base, also fitted out with classical columns. In between, the architect added a variety of decorations including triple windows in the attic story, minor pediments over corner bays, and a heavy cornice with modillions under widely projecting eaves.

The building is regularly attributed to J. E. Wilbanks as architect, but this is certainly a mistake. The Union County, Mississippi, courthouse is identical to Fayette's. The cornerstone in Union County reads: "Architect. H. E. Ostling, Montgomery, Ala." and below that, "John Wilbanks, Supt. of Bldg." The conclusion, then, is that the Fayette design is Ostling's and that Wilbanks was construction supervisor, perhaps even supervising architect in Fayette, although further information about Wilbanks's work has not been found.

The contractor in Fayette was the Little-Cleckler Construction Company from Anniston, one of the few Alabama building companies that developed its business beyond its home territory. Its record would eventually include courthouses and jails throughout Alabama, Georgia, and Mississippi.

County Court House.
...lville, Ala.

Geneva ↓   *Franklin* →

FRANKLIN COUNTY COURTHOUSE, RUSSELLVILLE (1892)

Architect: Fenton L. Rousseau; Builder: W. S. Hull (?)

Though the trade journal *Manufacturers' Record* reported in September of 1891 that Franklin County had adopted plans by Mississippi's William S. Hull, by December the county had selected Birmingham architect Fenton L. Rousseau (published as "J. Rousso") to design the county's courthouse in Russellville. The exterior of this imposing building reveals little of what goes on inside, except in the second-floor array of half-round arched windows that, without doubt, illuminated the courtroom. But what went on in an attic that features two levels of windows in the gable? The clock tower's elaborate decorations and the tall slender chimney pots underscore the building's vertical impression.

GENEVA COUNTY COURTHOUSE, GENEVA (1898)

Architect: Not recorded; Builder: James J. Johnson

Geneva County could tell one of the most heart-rending stories of courthouse destruction of any Alabama county. Fire destroyed the Geneva County courthouses built in 1888, and 1898; the courthouse of 1912 had fallen into an alarming state of disrepair before it was replaced and dismantled in the 1960s. This history is especially regrettable because these buildings were produced by some of Alabama's most talented designers and builders. The estimable M. M. Tye designed and built the Geneva County courthouse of 1888, the first "permanent"—that is, "brick"—courthouse. Sadly, it was not permanent, for it burned in 1896 and all the county's official records with it. Geneva County replaced Tye's building with the handsome structure of 1898 built by J. J. Johnson. Johnson was not, by profession, a building contractor, but a prominent businessman in Geneva with mercantile, cotton brokerage, and banking interests. Under his guidance, the very trim courthouse of 1898 rose, entered through an arcaded semi-recessed loggia surmounted by a pedimented portico supported by a pair of twin colonettes covering a balcony, an ensemble surely denoting the courtroom. Reigning over these embellished openings is a handsome bell and clock tower. Except for the cornice under the hipped roof, the rest of the building is unembellished. Overall, it might be identified by passers-by as "Neo-Colonial" and if that is adequate, few examples of the type outshine this simple one.

Heritage of Geneva County

GENEVA COUNTY COURTHOUSE, GENEVA (1912)

Architect: B. B. Smith; Builder: P. M. Metcalf

The awnings pictured in most photographs of the front of B. B. Smith's 1912 Geneva County courthouse, do not permit a confident reading of the design of the building. But stripped of the awnings the courthouse seems a more interesting—even if somewhat school-like— composition, perhaps even a precursor of Neo-Georgian style becoming popular. The greater interest in the design lies mostly in the skillful layering of tower elements. Rising from the slightly projecting entrance bay through a second-story door onto a balcony, a minor third story, and through an attic story to form a base for the tower, the corners of the next higher section are clipped and fitted with columns, further clipped in the next higher section to become an octagon, four sides of which have clock faces, and topped finally by an octagonal dome with lantern and finial.

The building contract was won by P. M. Metcalf, another prominent Geneva merchant and banker. A scathing, condemnatory complaint from the county bar association in the 1960s suggests that the design may have been inconvenient for effective upkeep of the building, or that county authorities were simply inattentive to it, or perhaps that its location in an area subject to flooding contributed to its deterioration. For whatever reasons, a new courthouse was built in a different location in Geneva and the old building was razed in 1966.

GREENE COUNTY COURTHOUSE, EUTAW (1869)

Builder: George M. Figh

On the ruins of Greene County's 1839 courthouse in Eutaw, destroyed shortly after the Civil War, builder George M. Figh erected in 1869 another courthouse of similar plan and proportions but not an exact copy of the old one, from specifications prepared by county authorities. Fortunately, a great deal of information about the 1839 building was available on which to base the reconstruction, in particular the detailed sketch of the courthouse that V. Gayle Snedecor included on his *Map of Greene County* in 1856. Contractor Figh worked pilasters into the stuccoed brick of the second floor, as found in the earlier courthouse, but the height of that story is greater than in the original building. Although brackets support the eaves all around, the architectural style of the building is comfortably Greek Revival. The hipped roof of the first courthouse appears here to have a shallower pitch than the original.

The interior plan on both floors reproduced the original. Broad crossing hallways divide the ground floor into four offices, with doorways on all four sides. Above the ground-floor entrances, the second-floor courtroom is given doorways with balconies of wrought iron (and an outside stair to the ground from the east balcony. This appears to make the arrangement of the original courtroom problematic. A solid wall with doors left and right of the judge's seat, seen in photographs of the 1930s, appears to have been a later addition.

HALE COUNTY COURTHOUSE, GREENSBORO (1869)

Architect: Unrecorded; Builder: Jesse Gibson, John Crossland

When the Alabama Legislature created Hale County in 1867, Greensboro's Salem Baptist Church, with wings added, became its first courthouse. Unlike the borrowed or rented spaces in which many new counties held their first courts, the church-turned-courthouse in Hale County was not considered temporary but planned for the long run. In fact, it served the county for almost forty years. The church was built about 1842, a careful example of Greek Revival style that one Greensboro history reports "was then considered the finest church edifice in west Alabama." The city of Greensboro bought the building from the Alabama Baptist State Convention in 1867, then donated it to Hale County in 1869.

The picture above shows the first of the building's wings to the right and its mirror twin added by the county to the left. Its hipped roof had a shallow enough pitch to fit under the entablature of the original classical building. The central arched entry suggests that this wing—and its twin later on the other side were divided into two offices each—quite adequate for a rural Alabama county in the mid-nineteenth century—and that the former church sanctuary became the courtroom. Surprisingly, however, the plan formed an "E" shape, for the wings were deeper at the extremes and shallower closer to the "courtroom." The rather grand bell/clock tower of the church had been removed, the large central window under the portico modified, and a second story of windows added under the portico, perhaps to let light into a gallery or jury rooms.

HALE COUNTY COURTHOUSE, GREENSBORO (1907)

Architect: H. E. Ostling; Builder: John A. Straiton

When the time came to replace its old church/courthouse, Hale County chose Montgomery architect H. E. Ostling (cf. Fayette County) to design a more modern facility and a local contractor, John Straiton, to build it. The courthouse opened in 1907 with lighting still provided by kerosene, but electricity was soon installed. Modern heating equipment was slow to be added; open grates were still used in 1925. So far as the neoclassical design goes, there is little to complain of nor to brag about. The conventional elements of designs in this mode are here, competently rendered and assembled. In a well-known Walker Evans Farm Security Administration photograph, the courthouse cupola can be seen towering over a Greensboro street of storefronts. The cupola seems almost out of place looking fresh and well-designed in contrast to storefronts that appear neglected, even unoccupied, afflicted, no doubt, with a Depression-era malaise. What cannot be entirely appreciated in that photograph, nor in the view presented here, is the impression of authority that is added to the design by the attic story of the building, even though the court building on its small lot seems crowded by its town neighbors.

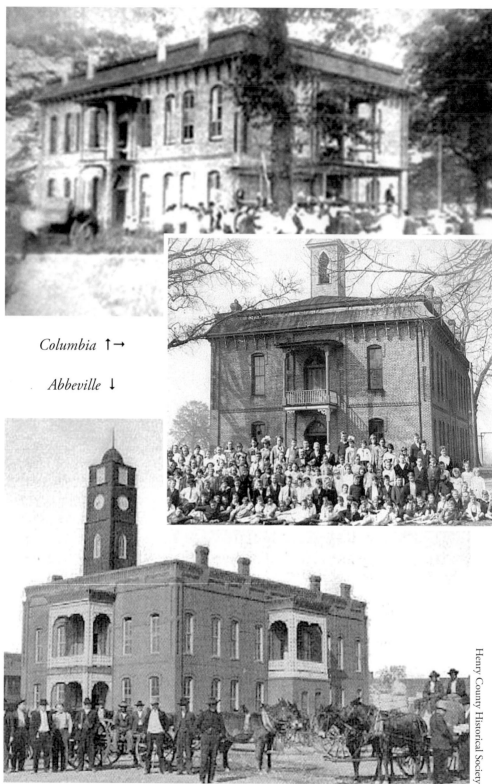

Columbia ↑ →

Abbeville ↓

Columbia Historical Society

Henry County Historical Society

Henry County Courthouse, Columbia (Unrecorded)

Architect: Unrecorded; Builder: John T. Jackson

Before Houston County was organized (1903), Columbia was still part of Henry County and served as county seat until Abbeville succeeded to that position. Assuming that the principal façade and main entrance was on the longer side of the building, the courthouse (top, facing page) appears to have been a nine-bay, double-pile, two-story building, with two-story porticoes on all sides, under a shallow mansard roof with closely spaced brackets under the eaves. Inside, hallways would have run from end to end and side to side of the first floor, and the courtroom occupied the second floor. Apparently, all the segmentally arched windows were protected by louvered blinds. For the time and place it was a fashionable public building. The center photograph on the facing page shows the short side of the building after it had been converted to a school.

Henry County Courthouse, Abbeville (1890)

Designer: Zacheriah Kirkland; Builder: Henry County Building Committee

If ever a building could be described as "ungainly," this one (bottom, facing page) surely could. Notwithstanding the filigree of the porches extending from its sides and segmental arches over its windows, there is little to save it from "homeliness," least of all its ill-proportioned clock tower. Zacheriah Kirkland was a Henry County native of some accomplishment in architectural design (see his First Methodist Church in Abbeville, for instance), but his talents deserted him here. The building committee that acted as contractor for the courthouse relied on John T. Jackson, who advertised himself as both builder and architect and who had built the Henry County courthouse at Columbia, to supply the bricks from his Abbeville brickyard and to supervise the masonry. With a constant eye on the cost of the building (only $8,000 in the end), the committee salvaged the stone foundation of the earlier courthouse for use in this building completed in 1890, just in time for the February court term but before the proper furniture had arrived.

To all appearances, the courthouse may have had a flat roof, though this would have been unusual in this period before roof sealants were reliable. Perhaps the camera angle just does not allow us to see a very shallow hipped roof and some sort of downspouting on the hidden sides of the building. Whatever the type of roof, it is well concealed from observation at street level by a low parapet, not unusual at this time, though usually troublesome for building maintenance.

Author's collection

HOUSTON COUNTY COURTHOUSE, DOTHAN (1905)

Architect: Andrew J. Bryan; Builder: M. T. Lewman & Co.

Andrew Bryan designed and the Lewman company built five distinctive courthouses on a three-part plan—an oval or round center section with rectangular front and rear sections. Two of these unusual courthouses were built in Alabama, one at Monroeville for Monroe County (*q.v.*) and the other, more elaborate one in Dothan for Houston County. (The others were in LaGrange, Georgia, Gulfport, Mississippi, and Minden, Louisiana.) Organized in 1903, Houston was the last county to be created in the state, so perhaps asserting newness by building an innovative and elaborate courthouse seemed fitting to the county fathers. Bryan's work was by this time well-known in Alabama, and execution of his plans would require an experienced builder such as the Lewman company, to handle the unusual circular form of the central (courtroom) section of the building, as well as the transitions between it and the front and rear rectilinear sections.

In the up-to-date city of Dothan, municipally supplied electricity came early and the new courthouse accordingly was wired to use this modern illuminating medium. Unfortunately, the city switched from the original direct current system to the even more up-to-date alternating current, while the courthouse was already invested in direct current equipment. Old photographs show electrical lighting appliances in offices but kerosene lamps on desktops. A true landmark in Dothan, the building nonetheless fell to a wrecker's ball in 1960 to be replaced by an undistinguished building in modern style that some citizens felt looked "incomplete." In the early years of the twenty-first century, the exterior of the building was substantially redesigned to mollify its earlier critics.

[Larger] *Early Courthouses of Alabama Prior to 1860*; [Inset] Author

JACKSON COUNTY COURTHOUSE, SCOTTSBORO (1868)

Architect: Unrecorded; Builder: Unrecorded

In 1868, the county seat of Jackson County was moved from Bellefonte, which had served since 1821, to Scottsboro following a spirited competition with three other sites for the honor. This small building was the first Jackson County courthouse in Scottsboro after the county seat was moved there. It is preserved today (without porch or framed addition) at the Jackson County Heritage Center Museum. Press reports of the time claim that county authorities immediately began building a county courthouse in Scottsboro. County records, however, had already been moved to that town before a new courthouse was completed. Whether the building shown here was purpose-built to be the courthouse or was acquired by the county after serving another use is not known. Local experts acknowledge that "courthouse" may be a misleading description of the building. Though "courthouse" was apparently the original description, "records office" may have been more fitting. In appearance recorded in this photograph, the building does not even give the impression of a purpose-built records office. More likely it was built for some other purpose, then adapted for records storage.

John R. Kennamer, *History of Jackson County*

JACKSON COUNTY COURTHOUSE, SCOTTSBORO (C. 1870)

Architect: Hiram Higgins; Builder: John D. Boren (perhaps "Warren")

Said to have been square in plan and 50'8" on each side, Jackson County's first substantial courthouse in Scottsboro used heavy brick pilasters with elaborate capitals of double brackets to outline this five-bay elevation (and perhaps sides and rear as well). The cupola is oddly designed and perhaps did not wear well with a critical public, for other photographs show a different-shaped roof atop its boxy base. The builder, (either Boren or Warren) came from Stevenson, a few miles upriver from Scottsboro. Hiram Higgins of Athens designed the courthouse here and the similar courthouses for Limestone and Lawrence counties, using paired brackets above the pilasters in Scottsboro but not in Moulton or Athens. Plans for all three buildings, however, are nearly the same. Of course, the Scottsboro cupola does not resemble anything on those two other buildings, but it had been changed several times, as already noted.

Corbis

JACKSON COUNTY COURTHOUSE, SCOTTSBORO (1912)

Architect: R. H. Hunt; Builder: Little-Cleckler

In early stages, planning for a new courthouse is seldom a smooth operation; none could have been less smooth than for Jackson County. False starts bedeviled the county from 1904 to 1911 when the *Birmingham News* was told: "This [the courthouse project] has been a troublesome question for several years. [The Little-Cleckler contract] is the third contract the county has made with contractors, all former contractors having failed to comply with the terms of their contracts." In addition, both B. B. Smith and Walter Chamberlin had prepared plans for various courthouse projects before construction finally began on the design of R. H. Hunt, Chattanooga's prolific and well regarded architect, Interestingly, the names of Jackson County commissioners inscribed on the courthouse cornerstone include architect F. L. Rousseau.

The notoriety that the Jackson County courthouse incurred as site of the early phases of the 1931 trial of the "Scottsboro Boys" (about which see also Morgan County courthouse) and an unimaginative expansion of the building in 1954, have obscured any very objective appreciation of the original building. Hunt, who was known to be a versatile designer, here showed the greatest restraint in presenting the classical revival in the simplest form. Aside from the tower, there is little ornamentation. The Tuscan order for portico and pilasters around the building was quite appropriate—approved for rural courthouses by no less an architectural critic than Thomas Jefferson.

JEFFERSON COUNTY COURTHOUSE, ELYTON (CA. 1841)

Architect and Builder: William Rose Sadler

William Rose Sadler had come to northern Alabama from Virginia to make his way as a builder. As part of his business, he created brick kilns in Elyton, near Birmingham, so that when the Jefferson County seat moved there from Carrollsville, he was ready to build the first brick courthouse for the county. The two views on the facing page depict the building about 1914, shortly before it was taken down.

The stairs to the upper floor show that the courtroom would have been located there. However, many questions about the structure remain unanswered. The roof is unusual, being gabled at one end and hipped at the other. Some features of the building—the front and side doors entering into the same inside space, for instance—suggest that it may have been built for or converted to commercial use, either before or after its civic use. On the other hand, the fine Flemish bond brickwork would be more usual for an original courthouse rather than a store.

Elyton's Jefferson County courthouse had been rebuilt after a fire in the 1870s, but as county seat it could not withstand the competition from nearby newly created Birmingham which, in 1873, became the new seat of Jefferson County.

In time Elyton was absorbed into Birmingham and the courthouse that William Rose Sadler built eventually disappeared.

Birmingham Public Library

JEFFERSON COUNTY COURTHOUSE, BIRMINGHAM (CA. 1875)

Architect: W. K. Ball; Builder: Frank Bugh & Co.; Frank P. O'Brien & Co.

The Italianate first Jefferson County courthouse to be built in Birmingham was certainly an appropriately stylish late-Victorian era addition to the cityscape. The design of the building is generally attributed to one W. K. Ball, though little is known of him. According to one letter-to-the-editor of the *Birmingham Age-Herald*, he was a Chicago architect. But just as likely he was the architect by that name practicing in Iowa during the 1870s. How he came to design for Birmingham is another of history's mysteries.

Although fire insurance maps tell us that the "dome [rose] about 60' over roof," the maps of this period do not reveal much about the interior arrangements in the building. One notation reads "Court Rooms 2nd [floor]." Perhaps the plural "Rooms" refers to jury and judges' rooms as well as the courtroom, for there seems not enough space for more than one courtroom. On entering the building from the street (Third Avenue) the visitor apparently passed under a part of the stairway that began about a third of the way down the entrance hall and wound up the left hall wall to a second-floor hallway.

Artwork of Scenes in Alabama

JEFFERSON COUNTY COURTHOUSE, BIRMINGHAM (1889)

Architect: Charles Wheelock & Sons, Henry Wolters; Builder: Charles Pearce

Architects for the massive 1889 Jefferson County courthouse were Charles Wheelock & Sons of Birmingham, in association with Henry Wolters of Louisville. The Wheelock firm had a substantial enough reputation that one wonders why an out-of-town architect was brought into the project. Part of the explanation may have been that Wolters was working with the contractor, Pearce, on an elaborate courthouse in Evansville, Indiana, and Wolters provided an entree to securing the services of Pearce.

Charles Pearce of Indianapolis was an important builder, the contractor for many county courthouses in Indiana including those for Vanderbrugh, Tipton, Clinton, Tippecanoe and Delaware counties in the 1880s and 1890s. He was best known for working in Indiana limestone (as all of the courthouses just mentioned were), but his work in Birmingham was in brick.

The Romanesque style building's180-foot clock tower was a successful rival to the spires of the Catholic Church next door, notwithstanding its somewhat anomalous Neo-Baroque appearance. (Notice the resemblance between the crown of the 1889 tower and that of the 1875 tower.) Visitors uniformly admired the building; locals thought it a fitting symbol of Birmingham's promise as the industrial center of the New South; photographers depicted it over and over. County authorities demolished it in 1937 and on another site replaced it with an enormous, uninspiring office building designed by Chicago's Holabird & Root.

Lamar County Genealogical and Historical Society

LAMAR COUNTY COURTHOUSE, VERNON (1870)

Architect: Unrecorded; Builders: Daniel J. Malloy & Jesse L. Taylor

Lamar County (in 1870 still named Sanford County) records date the completion of the first permanent courthouse in 1870. A substantial 1894 renovation of the building added four rooms. In view of the different window style of the pedimented wings, shown in this view, it may be that those wings date from 1894 and only the central portion of the building from 1870. In this photograph, the top of the center section of the façade is unfortunately obscured. The ox-eye window may be centered in an unpedimented gable, resembling some early Virginia courthouse styles (e.g., Fairfax), as would the arcaded entrance. But the round heads of second-floor windows and the arching brick decorative band above would be out of place in such a precedent.

LAMAR COUNTY COURTHOUSE, VERNON (1909)

Architect: Walter Chamberlin; Builder: B. C. Bynum Construction Co.

The charming, if somewhat quirky, Lamar County courthouse built in Vernon in 1909 survives today—so greatly disfigured as to be unrecognizable beneath an additional story, a "modern" façade in place of its portico, and a flat roof in place of its distinctive cupola.

Chamberlin's design seems competent so long as one's eyes do not linger too long over the columns, for then we would notice the absence of proper capitals and *entasis* and the use of odd banding on their bottom thirds. The cupola has no precedent in the classical canon, but suits the building, nonetheless. It sits on a battered (receding slope) base and is topped by a bell-shaped dome. Clearly, the Chamberlin formula here is not the often seen "office-floor-below/courtroom-floor-above" composition, for the projecting wings beside the portico would not have been part of the courtroom.

The contractor, B. C. Bynum, was an experienced Birmingham builder, known now particularly for having constructed the Shelby County courthouse (*q.v*) and the elaborate Smith Hall at the University of Alabama. Unfortunately, his 1909 work in Vernon has been obscured by the 1950 renovations in which a third floor was added to the building and its columns removed.

Artwork of Scenes in Alabama

LAUDERDALE COUNTY COURTHOUSE, FLORENCE (1822, 1850)

Architect: Unrecorded; Builders: James Pursell & Nathan Vaught

The first "permanent" courthouse for Lauderdale County was raised shortly after the county was created in the Alabama Territory and thus shortly before the Territory became the state of Alabama. Just as the town of Florence was created by land speculators, the courthouse in the town was part of their financial investment. The view above shows the 1850 enlargement of the simpler 1822 version that was square, with a hipped roof. The grand octostyle front porch of 1850 is apparently in a fluted Doric order with half columns as pilasters against the front wall of the building. Two sets of stairs provided access through two doors into the second-floor courtroom. Paired brackets were set under the eaves of the porch but not above the brick walls. At the rear of the building, a secondary entrance was within a recessed portico. Above the hipped roof, on a low square base, a square tower is composed of a lower almost cubic clock section, an octagonal lantern, and a small dome at the top. The building outlived its usefulness just as the nineteenth century closed, and even then, according to local tradition, parts of it were recycled for use in its successor (see *infra*).

University of North Alabama

LAUDERDALE COUNTY COURTHOUSE, FLORENCE (1901)

Architects: James W. Golucke & George W. Stewart; Builder: Neely & Smith

Even though the admired historian of the New South, C. Vann Woodward, claimed that the South "was too poor . . . to do much building in the period when architectural taste reached its lowest ebb" (*Origins of the New South, 1877–1913*), this building suggests that he exaggerated both the South's paucity of resources for building and the period's standards of taste. The proportions are excellent, the decorations restrained, and the octagonal tower neither over- nor underwhelming. Golucke's partner at the time was George W. Stewart, to whom alone the building is sometimes attributed. It is, however, clearly a Golucke design.

Histories of this building seldom fail to mention that the twelve columns of the previous Lauderdale courthouse were saved when the old building came down and reused for this 1901 building. However, the columns of 1901 were given Ionic capitals, unlike those of 1850.

The contract to build the Lauderdale courthouse was first won by Arthur Marshall who, newspapers reported, "jumped the job." But with the building scarcely begun, a new contract to complete it was given to Neely & Smith, a Chattanooga firm, who were essentially civil engineers with a record of projects for the Army Corps of Engineers. No other courthouses built by Neely & Smith are known.

Library of Congress

LAWRENCE COUNTY COURTHOUSE, MOULTON (1860)

Architect: Hiram Higgins; Builder: Unrecorded

The simplicity of the interior of the Lawrence County courthouse built in Moulton in 1860 was quite in keeping with the plain exterior. In the office spaces below and courtroom above, interior trim for door and window surrounds is plain (excepting the door to the records vault); heating is by fireplaces and stoves. The courtroom was arranged with jury facing the elevated judge's bench (rather than off to one side). A staircase leads from first to second floor and another from second floor to courtroom balcony.

The exterior of the building could almost be described as elegant in its simplicity. Architect Hiram Higgins divided each of the four equal sides into five bays. The repeating white window and door arches and pilaster bases and capitals punctuate the darker brickwork while the broad entablature unifies the composition.

Higgins, transplanted to Alabama from his native Kentucky, was an active antebellum designer in the area around Athens. He was an advocate particularly of the Greek Revival style. He was especially known for his domestic architecture, but he also designed academic buildings and at least three Alabama courthouses, in Lawrence County, seen here, and in Limestone and Jackson counties (*q.v.*).

Lee County Courthouse in 1880's (same site as present Courthouse)

Artwork of Scenes in Alabama

LEE COUNTY COURTHOUSE, OPELIKA (1869)

Designer and Builder: Horace King

Horace King built a reputation as a master builder of bridges. The record of his other building projects is not well documented, but in Lee County account books record his having been paid to build this courthouse, the first for the county shortly after it was created. King had come as a slave from South Carolina, so it is not surprising that he followed a South Carolina pattern in designing the Lee County courthouse, *i.e.*, double outside stairs to a portico entrance into the courtroom, with administrative offices underneath. Below the eaves and behind the portico the building has little embellishment, only shallow segmental arches (or perhaps shallow triangular arches) over the windows. Possibly to compensate, King placed brackets aplenty under the eaves. The photograph does not show capitals for the columns under the Doric entablature but proportions of the shafts seem right. The steps to the portico lying against the front wall were iron.

King's owner famously manumitted him through an act of the Alabama Legislature. As a freedman, King continued working as a bridge and building contractor from a home base in LaGrange, Georgia. Although he once bid for the contract to build a courthouse in Wetumpka for Elmore County, the Lee County courthouse is the only one in Alabama that can be definitely attributed to him.

COURT HOUSE, OPELIKA, ALA.

LEE COUNTY COURTHOUSE, OPELIKA (1898)

Architect: Andrew J. Bryan; Builder: Andrews & Stevens

By the time Lee County was ready to replace its first courthouse with a larger and more elaborate one, the architectural scene had developed far beyond what it had been when the county was created. Architectural training was more rigorous, both through apprenticeship and academic programs; extensive rail transportation facilities made movement of personnel and materials faster and more convenient; and the flow of information was greatly enhanced by the development of telephone and telegraph networks as well as by improved efficiencies in postal services that gave rise to vigorous suppliers of information in the form of architectural journals and building papers. Thus a young and ambitious Atlanta architect like Andrew J. Bryan could learn that Lee County would build a new courthouse, the Lee Countians could learn about him, he could envision such a building as he presented for their approval and, having secured a contract, his vision could in fact be produced. (See also Bryan's courthouses in Dale, Houston, Monroe, and Randolph counties.)

Virtually all the decorative elements that can be seen in this early photograph of the building are metal, mostly pressed metal, along with some cast metal elements, as in the Ionic capitals of the colonnade across the recessed portico. Catalogs of decorative metalwork were widely available; Bryan was likely an important patron of some of them, for this type work can be seen on a number of his courthouses (*e.g.*, the Muscogee County and Pulaski County courthouses in Georgia. A recent discovery of several apparently leftover pieces of this metalwork in the attic of the Lee County courthouse shows that the capitals were composed of eight separate pieces (four identical and another four their mirror images).

Just as is true for Bryan's remodeling of the Muscogee County courthouse (1896) in Columbus, Georgia, the influence of another building on the Lee County courthouse cannot be overlooked. That other building is the central portion of Walter T. Downing's Fine Arts Building at the Cotton States Exposition in Atlanta, itself probably directly influenced by the Fine Arts Building at Chicago's Columbian Exposition. Both at Columbus and Opelika, Bryan's designs include major features found in Downing's Fine Arts Building—an elaborately decorated frieze (though Bryan's were more restrained and not so wide as Downing's) and a recessed portico behind an Ionic colonnade. Curiously, the Fine Arts Building had seven columns, the Lee County courthouse, six, and the Muscogee County courthouse, five.

Perhaps the influence of Downing on Bryan is explicable by the fact that they were about the same age and both were practicing in Atlanta during the time these buildings were designed. (1895–96). While Downing had designed an important building for the Cotton States Exposition, Bryan also had a connection. As secretary (later president) of the Southern Institute of Architects, he was responsible for soliciting entries for an Exposition exhibit of architectural drawings—exhibited in the Fine Arts Building, one supposes.

The builders of this Lee County courthouse, Andrews and Stevens, were local operators of a planing mill and building supply business serving east Alabama. A disastrous fire proved an opportunity to expand their facilities and bring in more contracting business, although overexpansion may have been responsible for the eventual bankruptcy of the firm in 1902.

LIMESTONE COUNTY COURTHOUSE, ATHENS (1830S, 1869)

Architect and Builder: Hiram Higgins;
Rebuilding: Cyrus W. Crenshaw, Limestone County Commission

A near-twin of Kentuckian Hiram Higgins's Lawrence County courthouse (*q.v.*), the building familiar in postbellum photographs of the Limestone County courthouse is a rebuilding within the original walls of the structure built by Higgins in the 1830s. Invading Union forces had burned that building late in the Civil War. Many delays attended the rebuilding that the county commission itself supervised, so almost five years passed before the renewed courthouse was ready to be used; it then survived another forty-seven years.

Whether from affection or political gridlock, the county elders did not let go of the old building when it became clear that it needed to be replaced. In February 1909, the *Alabama Courier* observed, "The courthouse is still standing, notwithstanding its dangerous condition. It may continue to stand for some time to come." Indeed, it was not razed until 1916.

The photo below is another view of the one on the facing page, but shows more of the surrounding courthouse square.

Maurice Marlette

Alabama Department of Archives and History

LOWNDES COUNTY COURTHOUSE, HAYNEVILLE (1858)

Architect: Unrecorded; Builder: Unrecorded

Land speculators from South Carolina bought vast tracts of the Montgomery County lands later split off to become Lowndes County. Migrants largely from South Carolina settled there. South Carolina names, Lowndes and Hayne, were given to its two principal communities. And South Carolina style left its mark on the county courthouse, an outstanding example of the Greek Revival prototypes that Robert Mills and others had built across the Palmetto State. Of course, one's eyes are drawn to the portico and the curving stairs rising to it, a dramatic instance of the "open arms" effect in a public building. And every detail—flat stucco wall surfaces, pilasters, dentils, roof pitch—suggests that its unknown designer and builder and artisans were masters of the style and of their crafts.

In a misguided attempt to make the building more useful and "modern" in the early twentieth century, the county replaced the portico and stairs with a two-story office addition, added office wings at the sides, and an elaborate dome on the roof. In the 1980s, county residents and preservationists rallied support for a new renovation to return the exterior to very nearly its original appearance. Spaces for offices that had once been in the earlier side additions were placed instead to the rear, convenient to but not a part of the old courthouse. The dome, however, was left in place so visitors could mistakenly assume that it was part of the original building. Long-time Lowndes County residents will tell you that the dome has always leaked.

No records show that the design of the Lowndes County courthouse was influenced by the contemporaneous courthouse in Montgomery (*q.v.*). However, in view of the geographical proximity and the historical connection of the counties, and the fact that Montgomery's courthouse slightly predates Lowndes', that possibility ought not to be discounted.

MACON COUNTY COURTHOUSE, TUSKEGEE (1853)

Architect: Charles C. Ordeman; Builder: Unrecorded

The German-trained Montgomery architect Charles Ordeman designed courthouses for adjoining Macon and Montgomery counties, at about the same time. Their similarities are clear—second-floor courtroom entered from a classical portico reached by matching staircases curving from each side—the familiar "open arms" effect. Ordeman's design in Tuskegee was simpler than in Montgomery (*q.v.*) and in at least one respect unconventional. Surviving evidence is that at least one jury room was placed on the ground floor among county administrative offices, rather than on the upper floor adjacent to the courtroom, as was customary. The courthouse was picturesquely situated on an oval yard in the center of the town square, laid out so that the northwest and southeast sides are formed by through streets, while the northeast and southwest sides interrupt the perpendicular Main Street. The building's low-pitched hipped roof and absence of exterior decoration give a modest impression. On each side of the front door shallow recesses with semicircular heads are let into the wall. For the fluted columns of the portico, capitals are minimal and the entablature is shallow. As the county's fortunes declined, upkeep of the building declined as well. An early twentieth-century visitor observed that a deep layer of sand covered the floor in one downstairs room "to ameliorate the unevenness of the original brick, which is badly worn." Of the upstairs courtroom, he said, "Its most noticeable characteristic is its odor of nicotine."

An examination of the upper photograph draws one's attention to another "noticeable characteristic": though the eye is particularly drawn to the curving steps, the split louvered shutters on the upper-floor windows indicate that in all likelihood triple-hung sash were behind them. On the ground floor, however, were solid, paneled shutters in recognition of the security measures required in county offices.

Keith Vincent, *CourthouseHistory*

Macon County Courthouse, Tuskegee (1906)

Architect: J. W. Golucke; Builder: C. C. Totherow

For its 1906 courthouse, Macon County decided to face the town square from across the street. The building appears asymmetrical from the town square vantage, but it is bilaterally symmetrical. James Golucke designed it in the then fashionable style now referred to as Richardsonian Romanesque—that at least is suggested by the great double-arched front entrance of the building and the campanile-form tower. From the side, simply Romanesque might be adequate. The architect specified buff-colored brick, apparently unconcerned with its compatibility among the red brick of its neighbors around the square, or perhaps intentionally to make it stand out. Contractor C. C. Totherow, an experienced builder of jails and courthouses, had recently finished the Troup County courthouse in LaGrange, Georgia. The home base of his construction company is variously given as Montgomery or Birmingham. The efforts of its acclaimed architect and its experienced builder gave the Macon County courthouse a fortress-like appearance that suggested indestructibility. So it seemed until 1985 when some of the interior of the building was badly damaged by fire. Despite scarce resources, the county was able to return the building to its usual functions in 1991.

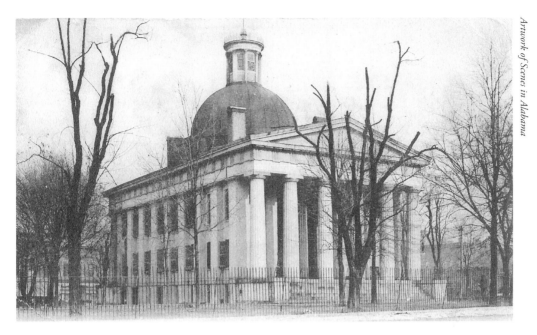

Artwork of Scenes in Alabama

MADISON COUNTY COURTHOUSE, HUNTSVILLE (1842)

Architect and Builder: George Steele

It is difficult to understand what could have impelled Madison County authorities to allow their 1842 courthouse to be taken down in 1913, particularly in view of the not so distinguished building that replaced it, to say nothing of the quite undistinguished building that replaced the replacement on the same site. George Steele, the designer and builder of this, the second Madison County courthouse, came early to Huntsville from Bedford County, Virginia, bringing with him a fine sense of the classical style that Thomas Jefferson was enthusiastically promoting in that part of Virginia.. Skilled in domestic architecture as well as public buildings, Steele contributed many fine homes to the Huntsville area.

Steele's conversion to the Greek (rather than Jefferson's Roman) Revival was apparently the fruit of a later visit to the Mid-Atlantic area. Particularly in this Madison County courthouse and in the First Alabama Bank, he captured the essence of the Greek temple style in monumental form. The courthouse had three full floors when the basement is included. As usual, the courtroom occupied the top story, offices below. The monumental Doric porticoes at opposite ends of the courthouse suited its location in the center of Huntsville's growing business district. Long sequences of pilasters along the building's flanks might have wearied an observer's eye, but that possibility was offset by the entablature with proper triglyphs running completely around the structure's four sides. The dome, lantern, and finial that Steele placed on the roof, though not precedented in Greek models, had long had a place in their revivals, particularly on governmental and ecclesiastical buildings.

MADISON COUNTY COURTHOUSE, HUNTSVILLE (1914)

Architect: C. K. Colley; Builder: Little-Cleckler

As early as 1897, the itch to replace George Steele's Greek Revival courthouse had struck the Madison County commissioners, for they had asked the prominent Louisville firm, McDonald Brothers, to prepare "plans for the county's proposed courthouse." Nothing came of that proposal, and for another fifteen years the courthouse stood undisturbed. But the commissioners began stirring again in 1912, when, on February 8, the *Manufacturers' Record* reported, "Madison County Commissioners will remodel and improve courthouse; will rebuild fronts, provide offices, etc." But the following week, February 15, it published this note: "Madison County Commissioners contemplate no repairs to courthouse as recently reported." However, a year later, after first advertising for plans and specifications to remodel the old courthouse, including adding two wings, the commissioners at last accepted plans by C. K. Colley of Nashville, for a new, fireproof 105' x 136' courthouse with steam heat and electric lighting. The Little-Cleckler Construction Co. of Anniston responded to the invitation to bid, won the contract, and built the new courthouse.

Architect Colley knew something about Greek Revival style, too, yet one hardly would gasp in delight when coming upon his courthouse as one might when coming upon Steele's. Colley gave his 1914 building four entrances under proper Doric porticoes, which made some sense for a building sitting in the middle of a city square already built up on all four sides. Little-Cleckler built the plan in light ochre brick and placed the clockworks from the old courthouse in the somewhat ungainly clock tower atop the new.

University of Alabama, Eugene Allen Smith

MARENGO COUNTY COURTHOUSE, LINDEN (CA. 1850)

Designer and Builder: Erastus Bardwell

Marengo County's mid-nineteenth century Greek Revival courthouse demonstrates just how thrilling the style can be. The order of the two great fluted columns of the portico is Doric employed in the simplest possible form, without any of the further embellishments that the order permits. The stuccoed street façade of the building contrasts attractively with the three brick wall surfaces lying behind it. The portico itself is notable; under the plain pediment and the plain entablature is a *distyle in muris* arrangement of features that provide support (columns), safety (railing on second-floor balcony), and access (stairs right and left rising to balcony; entrances to office floor below and courtroom above).

After the 1902 Marengo County courthouse was completed, the 1850 building was given over to a variety of uses, not all congenial to its dignified architecture. It once served for public betterment as a public school and later as a church, but at times more marginally as a riding stable, skating rink, and dance hall. Also it had a military life as National Guard armory and sometimes American Legion and Veterans of Foreign Wars lodge. The city of Linden is the present owner of the building, now only occasionally used for town meetings.

Little is known about Erastus Bardwell, listed in the 1850 U.S. Census as a carpenter. He came to Marengo County from the Connecticut Valley in Massachusetts, an area known for its enthusiasm for the Greek Revival. Bardwell was about forty-five when he built the county courthouse. He died just a year later. The Marengo County village of Jefferson was probably his home; he is buried there. Now a National Register Historic District, the town contains some fine Greek Revival buildings. Although a number date during Bardwell's years in the area, none has been confirmed as his work.

Keith Vincent, *CourthouseHistory*

Marengo County Courthouse, Linden (1902)

Architect: B. B. Smith ; Builder: Thomas Purvis

The architectural contrast between the 1850 classical Marengo County courthouse and that of 1902, usually described as Romanesque, illustrates a point about U.S. architectural fashion: it was not only a big-city or east coast/west coast phenomenon, but one attended to, at least among the decision-making set, in rural and agricultural settings.

Architect B. B. Smith prepared similar designs for Butler County and, in association with Frank Lockwood, for Baldwin and Escambia counties. With county approval, F. M. Dobson, who had built other Smith courthouse plans in south Alabama, transferred his contract for this one to Thomas Purvis, a move later involved in a tangled legal dispute (cf. *Marengo County, et al. v. Thomas D. Matkin,* 144 Ala. 574).

In appearance the building looks substantial enough to resist the harshest threats and, indeed, it did—lightning strikes and a tornado. But it was not fireproof and could not resist flames that damaged it beyond repair in 1965. Fireproof records storage was apparently not a part of B. B. Smith's design, but fortunately an addition, noted on the fire insurance map as "Vault Fireproof Constr." had been added sometime before 1933, so most of the county's records were preserved.

Author's collection

MARION COUNTY COURTHOUSE, PIKEVILLE (1820?)

Architect and Builder: Unrecorded

County histories maintain that this was the courthouse built when Pikeville was chosen to be the first permanent Marion County seat. In 1859, it became the home of Judge John Dabney Terrell Sr., and of a succession of tenants afterward—thus, its domestic rather than civic appearance. A watercolor view of the house, dated about 1910, shows that an earlier front porch was only one-story.

Copy of watercolor courtesy of Robert Gamble

Sabra N. Sudberry

MARION COUNTY COURTHOUSE, HAMILTON (1883, 1889)

Architect: Unrecorded, Frank Allen; Builders: John D. Hise, John C. Camp

In April 1882, the building paper, *Carpentry and Building*, included one item that gave some sketchy information about the early Marion County courthouse:

> A FRAME COURTHOUSE, 42 x 75 feet, a stone jail, and a jailor's residence, are under contract at Toll Gate [later Hamilton], Marion Co., Ala. Mr. John D. Hise of Bel Green, same state, is the contractor.

Unfortunately, Mr. Hise's courthouse burned to the ground at the end of March 1887. Another, also of frame construction, was built on the same site. County residents claim* that the photograph above is of one of those buildings under construction, but it is not clear which one and in any case the building type seems quite un-courthouse-like. The *Marion Herald* reported in February 1888 that "Mr. J. T. White is putting up the pillars for the new court house this week." Would the building shown have had pillars? Framework depicted for some sort of double-deck porch would require some type of support. The question remains open, for Hise's building may have had "pillars" as well.

*See, for example, http://theusgenweb.org/al/marion/courthouse.htm.

Marion County Historical Society

Marion County Courthouse, Hamilton (1902)

Architect: Unrecorded; Builder: (F. M. Dobson) Alabama Jail and Bridge Company

Regrettably, the name of the architect who designed the 1902 Marion County courthouse in Hamilton has been lost, for it was an interesting design. It also is regrettable that, although the building still stands, it has almost completely disappeared behind and underneath additions and alterations over the years.

Built of coursed rubble—perhaps the native sandstone available in the area—and covered by an unexpectedly steeply pitched hipped roof, the building had several features that stand out. One was the clock tower that, unlike many other courthouses of this time, does not soar, but neither is it squat; perhaps "substantial" best conveys its character. Another feature was the Romanesque arch framing the recessed doorway. And yet another was the design of the second-floor windows; they appear quite narrow for their height (although the same width as the first-floor windows). In all likelihood, each is two separate windows, the recessed spandrel indicating the floor level of a gallery above the courtroom.

The experienced contractor F. M. Dobson had incorporated his business as the Alabama Jail and Bridge Company, and under that name was a party in the case, *Alabama Jail & Bridge Co. v. Marion County,* 145 Ala. 684, involving "damages caused by the workman's breach of contract in the performance of the work."

Marshall County Online

MARSHALL COUNTY COURTHOUSE, GUNTERSVILLE (1870)

Architect: Unrecorded; Builder: Unrecorded

As Marshall County recovered from the devastation of the Civil War, it built this courthouse to replace the log structure that had been destroyed along with almost everything else in Guntersville. In this photograph, it appears as a thoughtfully designed public building with Greek Revival touches such as its temple form and pilasters. There is nothing careless about the side elevations, for which the pilasters define the five bays, nor about the windows' nine-over-nine sash, shutters upstairs but not downstairs, and whitened lintels and sills. We have no explanation for the substitution of bricked-in frames on the first-floor entrance porch rather than actual windows. There seems no reason to omit windows on the porch downstairs but provide them upstairs.

The front of the building is not nearly as appealing as its sides, seeming dark and mysterious rather than open and welcoming. Despite that, the balustrade across the entire upper porch is an attractive feature. Less successful but serviceable are the square brick piers supporting the second-floor porch and the gable above. Especially to be regretted is the absence of a more defined horizontal base to make the gable end into a proper pediment. Notwithstanding, the design is a considerable achievement in what was then an isolated rural location. For that reason, it is especially disappointing that we have not yet identified the designer and builder.

Marshall County Court House,
Guntersville, Ala.

Keith Vincent, *Courthouse History*

MARSHALL COUNTY COURTHOUSE, GUNTERSVILLE (1896)

Architect and Builder: Edward M. Wallen

Marshall Countians decided in the 1890s that the time had passed for the Greek Revival style and their simple courtroom-over-office-floor courthouse; they tore down the old one and replaced it with a much larger building. With a bow to the popular Romanesque Revival style, the design included an arcuate entry that, judging from the door above it, could be used for addressing a public gathered in the courtyard. Also from the Romanesque are the rounded window openings. However, the attention-grabbing tall tower, with steeply pitched octagonal roof, that dominates the building is not Romanesque at all and seems incongruous with the collection of elements below it.

Edward M. Wallen, an architect whose office was in New Decatur, was awarded the building contract at $20,000, so the assumption is that he both designed and supervised the construction. Sadly, he did not have long to enjoy whatever plaudits the building earned. In its issue of March 7, 1897, the *New York Sun* reported: "Edward M. Wallen, an architect of New Decatur, Ala., was found dead in his room at the St. Nicholas Hotel, Broadway and Washington Place, at noon yesterday. Heart disease is supposed to have caused his death."

He was about forty-five years old.

T. J. Carnes, *Out of the Sand*

MARSHALL COUNTY COURTHOUSE, ALBERTVILLE (1911)

Architect: H. D. Breeding; Builder: H. M. Johnson

Although Albertville was never the Marshall County seat, a courthouse has operated there since 1911 and continues there today (see *Alabama Local Acts* 1919, no. 23, p. 14). The impetus for this arrangement was the occasional flooding of the Tennessee River that effectively cut off the citizens of Albertville and the surrounding parts of Marshall County from Guntersville, the county seat, when they wished to do business at the county courthouse.

Although county histories assert that the courthouse was built just for that purpose, the only known photograph of the original Albertville courthouse suggests that the courthouse portico may have been added to an original stepped front that would have seemed more appropriate for a commercial building. The stepped parapet does not appear to align with the planes of the front and side walls, suggesting that a later layer covering of some material was applied to the original walls.

Circuit court sessions had been convened in Albertville since the late 1800s, apparently not in a purpose-built courthouse. However, on "a beautiful corner lot, near Main Street," with funds raised by Albertville citizens, the first courthouse in Albertville was conveyed to Marshall County on December 27, 1911.

MOBILE COUNTY COURTHOUSE, MOBILE (1872)

Architect: W. O. Pond; Builder: Charles Fricke

W. O. Pond, who designed the Mobile County courthouse of 1872, was one of those individuals whose role on the building scene morphed from carpenter to "contractor" to "architect" after he came to Alabama from South Carolina. As contractor, he was responsible for erecting several of the designs of J. H. Hutchison, the Reconstruction-era Mobile architect and member of the distinguished Hutchison family of architects in the years following.

When the Austrian immigrant Charles Fricke received the contract to construct the fine substantial classical courthouse portrayed above, his reputation as a builder was already secure. He had worked for James Freret at Spring Hill College, and in the same year that he completed the courthouse he finished construction of Mobile's Bernstein-Bush House (now Mobile's Mardi Gras Museum) that Hutchinson had designed. Fricke was something of an innovator, having received an 1860 patent for "Improved Cement," a composition of "hydraulic cement, pozzolona, coarse sand, tar, and tallow."

The drawing shown here of its classical façade is the only available image of the 1872 courthouse. But Fricke must have built it well, for after the fire that destroyed the building in 1888, a new courthouse was built on the old foundation and within the old first-floor walls.

University of South Alabama

MOBILE COUNTY COURTHOUSE, MOBILE (1889)

Architect: Rudolph Benz; Builder: Louis Monin

Mobile architect Rudolph Benz displayed originality in crowning his essentially classical 1880 Mobile County courthouse with extensive Victorian bric-a-brac on the roof. A regular series of fires had bedeviled Mobile's courthouses, including the immediate predecessor of Benz's building. That predecessor (Mobile County courthouse of 1872) was a very correct classical temple building. Perhaps Benz was referring to the old with a classical choice, but, as Robert Gamble has written in his *Alabama Catalog*, "the statuary-studded roofline was more attuned to the bourgeois Neo-Renaissance taste of . . . Benz's native Stuttgart." The sculptural pediment was another part of the decorative ensemble, but the solid shutters at the first-floor windows were a matter of expediency. Security was ever on the minds of courthouse designers and builders; one response was to install solid first-floor shutters on courthouses in a variety of styles.

In 1906, tornadic winds destroyed what Benz had placed on the roof. Rebuilding that part of the building and altering other features—window and corner trim, for example—produced a more sober, businesslike appearance at the expense of Benz's confectionery.

Monroe County Heritage Museum

MONROE COUNTY COURTHOUSE, MONROEVILLE (1852)

Architect: Unrecorded; Builder: J. W. Perrin

The substantial brick courthouse in these photographs replaced the 1830 first courthouse in Monroeville. At one postbellum point, the 1852 courthouse featured a cast iron double exterior stair, requiring that two first-floor windows behind the stairs be bricked up, as can be seen in this photograph. The building does not offer the stylishness of its successor, but a clue to an improving economic condition of the county may be the windows that feature 12-over-12 sash and shutters on both floors.

Monroe County Heritage Museum

MONROE COUNTY COURTHOUSE, MONROEVILLE (1903)

Architect: Andrew J. Bryan; Builder: M. T. Lewman & Co.

A. J. Bryan's Monroe County edifice is perhaps the best-known courthouse in Alabama because it was the model for the one in Harper Lee's popular novel, *To Kill a Mockingbird.* Like his Houston County courthouse (*q.v.*), it combined three volumes in a way that no other architect either could have or would have wanted to imitate, and he wrapped the composition in a neoclassical finish. The first section was planned as three arms of a Greek cross with entrances to the building at both corners nearest the street. The middle section was an elliptical cylinder. A courtroom with gallery occupied the second floor, while on the first floor of this section a smaller oval room in the center is flanked by curved walkways on both sides to fill out the cylinder's shape and permit a patron to move from front section to rear section without entering the central oval space. The rear component of the building, of rectangular plan, provided judges' chambers and jury rooms. Prisoners to be tried or examined as witnesses were brought from the jail behind the building through a rear entrance in this section and held in secure facilities there.

The Bryan collaboration in Monroeville with contractor M. T. Lewman & Co. was one of many in Alabama and the southeastern states. (See Coffee County, Dale County, and Houston County, *supra.*) The dome that Lewman built for the Monroeville courthouse is typical of many of his later buildings. Vertical ribs were fashioned from short pieces of dimension lumber and braced horizontally, much in the manner of the famous Delorme dome developed in France. Inserted into the large domed cupola at the center of the Greek Cross was the obligatory clock, and beneath the dome was the obligatory courthouse bell (cast by Baltimore's McShane Bell Foundry, as many courthouse bells across the country were).

Image; Library of Congress; Sketch, Robert Gamble

MONTGOMERY COUNTY COURTHOUSE, MONTGOMERY (1838)

Architect: Unrecorded; Builder: John P. Figh

This, the only known early image of the 1838 Montgomery County courthouse, appeared on the cover of a sheet music edition of a popular tune, "Owen's Quick Step," dedicated to the military group, the Montgomery True Blues. The building to the left, above, has been identified as the courthouse, a very trim classical temple building with what seem to be excellent proportions for the style. Around 1830, the builder, John Figh, had come from Maryland to Tuscaloosa, working there on some of the University buildings. By 1835, he had moved on to Montgomery, where he received the contract to build the 1838 county courthouse. Since Figh owned a brickyard, he surely built the courthouse of brick, possibly even the columns, though plastered over. Otherwise the trim would have been wooden, painted white. The location was on Court Square, so named for the location of the first Montgomery County courthouse, though after this, the second county courthouse, no subsequent courthouses were built here.

Alabama Department of Archives and History

Montgomery County Courthouse, Montgomery (1854)

Architect: Charles C. Ordeman; Builder: Bird F. Robinson & Erastus Bardwell

In 1852, Montgomery County called on Charles C. Ordeman, the German immigrant architect who also designed the courthouse in adjoining Macon County (*q.v.*), to create its new courthouse. It might be said that this (and many others) was a courthouse that ego built, at least that was the opinion of many correspondents to local newspapers and public protesters. The earlier courthouse down on Court Square, proponents of a new building thought, was too small or at least not grand enough for the capital city of the state. Then, too, that could be a prime downtown spot for commercial development.

But even as complaints continued, a new site was acquired, Ordeman prepared plans, and the Montgomery contracting partnership of Robinson & Bardwell, who had already built the Alabama State Capitol, was hired to build the Greek Revival temple that became the Montgomery County courthouse. Its double curving stairs up to the portico were a major design feature, as was the rustication of the first floor, entered under the portico and fading into the grade toward the rear of the site.

Carping did not end with the move into the new courthouse. Complaints ranged from bad design (a fireplace behind the judge's bench) and poor acoustics, to construction flaws (leaky roof). Nonetheless, the building stood for forty years and, at the end of that time, proved to be too good simply to demolish when Montgomery's need for a large courthouse developed. Thus . . . (see *infra*).

Artwork of Scenes in Alabama

MONTGOMERY COUNTY COURTHOUSE, MONTGOMERY (1893)

Architect: McGrath & Walker; Builder: Unrecorded

. . . Thus (see *supra*), McGrath & Walker, the architects of the 1893 Montgomery County courthouse, incorporated the 1854 building into the 1893 building. The three left-most bays of the building pictured above retained the gable in the roof but shed the portico and double stairway on the front of the original building. What was not evident from the front of the building was that the plan was U-shaped. However, the building was the same depth at every part of the façade except at the central tower block. Behind that part of the building was the narrow opening of the U, separating relatively fat "arms." About 1930, this feature was closed in. A screen of four Corinthian columns across the face of the original left section of the building matched another set of four on the extreme right section, and joined four more above the central entrance to the expanded courthouse. An imposing two-stage tower capped by an ogival roof dominated the entire composition.

William Thomas Walker had come to Montgomery in 1873. He had left his native New York to recover his health in California before returning to the east coast and finally Montgomery, where he advertised himself in the Montgomery City Directory as "W. T. Walker, Carpenter, Builder and Architect," with an office on Lawrence Street, also the location of the courthouse. His partner, McGrath, was either Charles E. or Robert N. McGrath, a father-son team who appeared in the 1891 Montgomery City Directory as "architects" with an office on Dexter Avenue.

Morgan County Archives

MORGAN COUNTY COURTHOUSE, COTACO (PRE-1820)

Architect: Unrecorded; Builder: Unrecorded

The first recorded sessions of the Cotaco (later Morgan) County Court were held in this building, often referred to as the "White House," in the village of Cotaco. The structure was, not surprisingly, an example of the adaptation of buildings that could serve a newly created county's needs until a purpose-built courthouse could be constructed. The most current information is that the building was the site of only the first two-day session of the Cotaco County Court, meeting in June of 1818. The White House, in this case, was possibly a family home, but considering its size and the arrangement of interior spaces, probably a tavern or inn. Cotaco County was created by the Territorial Legislature so the building would have been built slightly before Alabama became a state. A substantial renovation of the building was undertaken in the 1980s.

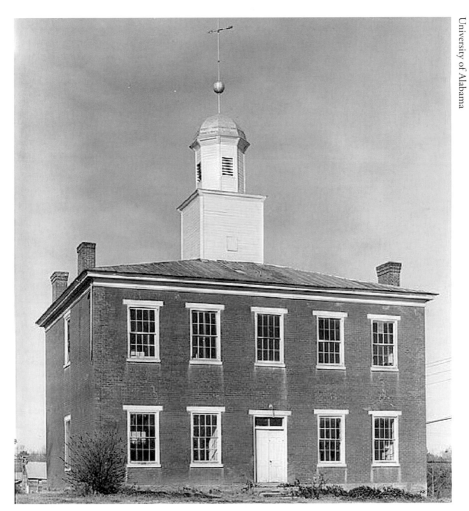

University of Alabama

MORGAN COUNTY COURTHOUSE, SOMERVILLE (C. 1837)

Architect: Unrecorded; Builder: Unrecorded

A more straightforward utilitarian structure than this early Morgan County courthouse is difficult to conceive. It was built in the village of Somerville about 1837. Except at the top of the cupola where the octagonal and domed belfry sits, everything is quite plain, and very striking because of that. Can we suppose the builders were reaching for "Federal" style, as the building is sometimes described? Some of the interior woodwork is "Federal," but what one sees outside may be interpreted more simply in terms of "utility" and "economy" rather than "style": large windows provided necessary light to offices and courtroom room; sash with eight-over-eight lights were used because large panes of glass were not available and/ or affordable; flat arches were more easily constructed than alternate forms; paint protected the wood of which arches and sills were constructed; the transom over the front door lit the hallway; the shallow hipped roof required less lumber.

Alabama Department of Archives and History

MORGAN COUNTY COURTHOUSE, DECATUR (1893)

Architect: Walter Chamberlin; Builder: Lawrenson & Wallen

Walter Chamberlin placed his signature belfry and clock tower on the roof of the Morgan County courthouse he designed when the county seat was moved from Somerville to Decatur. Characteristically, he also placed pyramidal roofs on the square corner protrusions all around the building. (See Crenshaw County and Dallas County, *supra*.)

Contractor David Lawrenson had arrived in Morgan County after leaving his native Canada to settle for a while in North Dakota before heading south to Alabama. His partner, Edward M. Wallen, was often a collaborator with architect Chamberlin. As he was about to complete his work in Decatur, Wallen (see Marshall County, *supra*), was awarded a contract to build a Chamberlin-designed courthouse in Macon County, Georgia—less elaborate than Morgan County's new building, but with the same signature features. In the next year, Wallen was building the Washington County courthouse in Johnson City, Tennessee.

Jenkins & Knox, The Story of Decatur

MORGAN COUNTY COURTHOUSE, DECATUR (1928)

Architect: Bem Price; Builder: Not recorded.

The Morgan County courthouse is included in this collection because it was an important venue in Alabama legal history—even though it is not properly a "vintage" structure. To this building were transferred later phases of the Scottsboro Boys trials, lasting from 1933 to 1937.

It is said that the courthouse was built upon the ruins of its burned predecessor, and a comparison of the Sanborn map images of the 1893 and 1928 buildings shows that this may well be the case. Extensions to left and right of the main block and additions to the rear, including an attached jail, expanded the building greatly, but the first-floor plan of the older courthouse, including its wide, crossing first-floor corridors, was retained in the newer one. The Birmingham architect Bem Price, known for neoclassical designs, placed paired columns at the main entryway and alternating triangular and segmental window pediments above the matching three windows of the projecting ends of the façade. These features lent some classical feeling to the new building, replacing the Victorian impression of the old.

Following the demolition of the building in 1976, its grounds became a park adjacent to the present county courthouse.

PERRY COUNTY COURTHOUSE, MARION (1856)

Architect: Benjamin F. Parsons; Builders: James Didlake & Larkin Y. Tarrant

By the middle of the nineteenth century, when Black Belt cotton underpinned Perry County wealth and thriving educational institutions underpinned its sense of importance, a new courthouse was undertaken, perhaps in hopes of displaying those qualities to neighbors far and wide. Around 1850 from Massachusetts had come Benjamin F. Parsons, a carpenter/architect who knew just what the case demanded, a grand Greek Revival temple. While it may have seemed to his clients that Parsons was playing to Old South sensibilities, with a bow to academic architectural precedent, more likely his inspiration came from the colon-naded temples he remembered from his early New England years. By the 1850s Parsons had many examples of classical hexastyle porticoes to inspire him, many using Ionic capitals, such as Jefferson's influential Virginia State Capitol. Porticoes at both ends of the building (*amphiprostyle*) were sure to capture public attention. And so, too, were the "bows" in the building's sides, not true apses even though semicircular, for they did not terminate an aisle nor a courtroom, nor were they vaulted. They were, somewhat prosaically, accommodations for stairs between floors, an idiosyncratic feature, regrettably now removed. The out-of-scale belfry atop the portico is probably a later add-on.

Pickens County Courthouse, Carrollton (1877)

Architect and Builder: Fenton L. Rousseau

The Pickens County courthouse is well known for the "face in the window," said to have been permanently etched in the glass of an attic pane. But for all its renown, little is recorded of those who built it, or more accurately, "rebuilt" it on the foundations of the older courthouse that burned. According to one of two common local stories, the older building burned at the hands of an arsonist, possibly the man whose face was etched into the newer building's attic windowpane by a lightning strike, just as he was taken from the room to be executed.

For reasons not at all clear, specifications for this Pickens County courthouse have been found in the Elmore County courthouse. The heading of this document reads, "Specifications: For Material and Work to be done in the construction of a Court House to be built in the city of Wetumpka, County of Elmore, and State of Alabama." However, at the end of the document, is a certification by the Pickens County Probate Judge that the specifications are those adopted by the Pickens County Commissioners Court, with references to the Deed Book in which they were recorded. The Elmore County courthouse of 1885 (*q.v.*) does bear a slight resemblance to this one in Carrollton, so perhaps the later was in some way modeled on the earlier. In both, bracketed cornices and elongated arched windows give a provincial Italianate flavor.

Holman Johnson, Pike County Remembered

PIKE COUNTY COURTHOUSE, TROY (1881)

Architect: G. J. Ferris; Builders: Fox Henderson & Joseph Minchener

The prominent Troy businessman Fox Henderson and his partner Joe Minchener were the contractors for the Pike County courthouse of 1881, the first the county built in brick. The building's appearance was transformed a number of times. While at times described as "square," in neither this nor other period photographs nor in Sanborn map representations of it does the courthouse appear to have been so. Other descriptions include front and back porticoes, possibly later additions, for this photograph does not show any portico. Perhaps to add some "style" to an otherwise plain building, the architect or the builders added brackets at the eaves and hood molds to the segmentally arched windows. Other than the proportions, the principal feature confirming that the Pike County courthouse of 1898 incorporated this one of 1881 is those window arches (see below).

PIKE COUNTY COURTHOUSE, TROY (1898)

Architect: R. L. Jones; Builder: McAfee & Co.

One must look closely to see that the Pike County courthouse of 1898 is the 1881 version with additions and alterations. To the 1881 building, four square corner pavilions were added. Although period photographs do not show both the east and west entrances to the building, the footprint shown on town maps suggests they were identical. Between the pavilions of both east and west elevations, the architect designed a recessed, two-tiered portico having an arcaded entrance below and a pedimented Ionic portico above. Atop the original part of the structure is the customary bell and clock tower, featuring outsized clock faces. As noted previously (*supra*), the window arches of the 1881 building were evident in Pike's courthouse of 1898, but were not reproduced in the corner pavilions

Other than a school building in Walker County, no other Alabama designs by Atlanta architect R. L. Jones are known. Likewise, only one other Alabama building is known to have been erected by Atlanta contractor McAfee & Co. during this period, a dormitory for the Girls' Industrial School at Montevallo (now University of Montevallo).

Randolph Leader

Randolph County Courthouse, Wedowee (1897)

Architect: Andrew J. Bryan; Builder: N. B. McPherson

Citizens complained that A. J. Bryan, the architect chosen by the Randolph County commissioners to design a courthouse to replace one that had burned in 1896, was not present in Wedowee often enough to oversee the new building and that it was coming along much too slowly as a result.

Their impatience hardly seems reasonable in view of the completion of the courthouse within a year. But there is little doubt that Bryan was an infrequent visitor to the project for he was busily traveling widely to drum up new business, not only in Alabama (see Houston County, Lee County, Dale County) and in his home state of Georgia but in Mississippi and Louisiana as well. However, the builder had a sound local reputation and the design pleased the Randolph County patrons.

In the local newspaper, comments focused on the clock tower and belfry and regular reports were published about its progressive rise into the sky. Notwithstanding the commissioners' requirement that the building be fireproof, in 1940 it was destroyed by fire, just as its predecessor had been.

RUSSELL COUNTY COURTHOUSE, SEALE (1868, 1908)

Architect: John Lewis (1868), T. F. Lockwood (1908); Builder: Simeon O'Neal (1868), E. C. Seiz (1908)

The seat of Russell County, originally at Girard, moved to Crawford (Crockettsville), and then to Seale, thought to be the center of the county. No images of the original courthouse built in Seale are known, but in 1907–08, the county engaged T. Firth Lockwood, who had moved away from Montgomery (and from his brother Frank's thriving architectural practice) to Columbus, Georgia, just across the river from Russell County, to renovate its courthouse. Lockwood turned the old courthouse into this impressive classical building that served the county until the county seat moved once more in 1935, this time to Phenix City, the population center but far from the geographical center of the county. The building in Seale was designated a branch courthouse until that service, too, was discontinued in 1943. Though the design may be considered unimaginative, it is well-proportioned, suited to its site on a rise above the town, and not offending anyone's idea of what a rural county courthouse ought to look like. Lockwood's only bow to external embellishment was in the gable ornament and the style of the splayed lintels over windows and doors, including the small windows at the top of the second story that gave light to the gallery above the courtroom. Occasionally this space was used as a basketball court after the county officers decamped for Phenix City and abandoned the building.

Simeon O'Neal, a Seale resident, was the contractor for the original courthouse and later became probate judge of Russell County. Of architect John Lewis, nothing has been learned. Because part of the work of Lockwood and Seiz in 1908 was "bricking up" the old building, just what their work entailed is not certain. Unless the original building was frame and a brick covering was added, "bricking up" may refer to adding a brick veneer to an already brick building, or, as some suggest, removing and replacing the original outer layer of brick and replacing it with finer brick and matching-color mortar. The uniform dark color of the building today may suggest the latter. Although E. C. Seiz was himself an architect, it was to his Atlanta building company that Lockwood awarded the contract for alterations to the courthouse in Seale.

Shelby County Historical Society

SHELBY COUNTY COURTHOUSE, COLUMBIANA (1854, 1881)

Architect: McCan & Williamson; Builder: Unrecorded

The first courthouse in Columbiana was a converted school building, replaced in 1854 with a purpose-built frame courthouse that was the bones of the rear portion of the building shown here. No photograph of the structure as it first served is known. When the building was expanded in 1881 to include brick additions to the front and to the rear, the original frame portion was clothed in brick to match. Above is the earliest known photograph of the whole ensemble, but pictured as the hotel it became when a new courthouse was built on another site. In much improved appearance, it now is home to the Shelby County Historical Society, the county museum and archives. Some describe its style as "Italianate" despite the plaque in front of the building that identifies its style as "classical Jeffersonian." Jefferson might demur. The conclusion perhaps should be that architectural "style" is often in the eye of the beholder

No Alabama county has a more tangled courthouse history than Shelby County, yet some of the confusion had nothing to do with this building in Columbiana. In keeping with a rather odd interpretation of the legal precept known as Dillon's Rule—that inferior legal jurisdictions such as counties are creatures of the state and thus the state government is entitled to do just about anything it wishes within an Alabama county—the state legislature decided that another courthouse and jail should be built (at Shelby County's expense) and that it must lie on the route of the Central of Georgia Railway. Bowing to the legislature's wishes, and following a contentious competition, the county chose Calcis as the site.

The Manufacturers' Record announced in July 1902 that Walter Chamberlin would prepare plans and specifications for the new courthouse and jail. In August the *Montgomery Advertiser* reported, "The contract for the erection of the courthouse and jail at Calcis was let this week, M. C. Banks having bid it off at $9,900 complete, including the cells in the jail." Despite all this, no courthouse was built in Calcis. Described today as an unincorporated community, the town is a small collection of buildings at a Shelby County crossroad, next to railroad tracks.

Shelby County Historical Society

SHELBY COUNTY COURTHOUSE, COLUMBIANA (1908)

Architect: Bruce Architectural Co.; Builder: B. C. Bynum Construction Company

Another tangle ensnared Shelby County's courthouse history with the competition between the antebellum seat of Columbiana and the postbellum railroad town of Calera for the designation as county seat. Court battles were involved (see *Brown v. Shelby County; Farson, Son & Co. v. Bird, Treasurer*). Columbiana won. There the Bynum Construction Company built the new and much larger county courthouse that Alexander Bruce, the Atlanta architect, had designed. Many of Bruce's Georgia buildings have been described as "picturesque," presumably referring to their eclectic character but also to a pleasing quality in the assemblage. In Columbiana, the assemblage may be a bit more jarring than picturesque, but certainly it is not "dull."

Bynum built the walls of the Shelby County courthouse with twelve inches of brick on the first floor, eight inches of brick on the second, and faced with a four-inch ashlar stone veneer over the brick, according to the first Sanborn fire insurance map to record the building in 1909. In plan, the building was symmetrical with projecting pavilions. A monumental portico with composite columns on plinths sheltered the main entrance, and small porticoes marked the building's side entrances. Above the eaves, a balustrade, interrupted by the front pediment, surrounds the roof, and above each of the projecting corner rooms, Bruce placed hemispherical domes. An elaborately devised clock tower with dome rises above the "collection" below.

Keith Vincent, *CourthouseHistory*

ST. CLAIR COUNTY COURTHOUSE, PELL CITY (1903)

Architect: Walter Chamberlin; Builder: Robert P. Manley

The "other" St. Clair County courthouse in Pell City recognizes a geographical reality—that Backbone Mountain divides the county in two. Though that division was more inconvenient at a time when transportation and communication were far more difficult than today, occasional efforts to consolidate county seats, courthouses, or judicial districts have thus far failed to dislodge the old dual system.

County voters selected the second county seat through a competitive county election according to the terms of an ordinance under the 1901 Alabama Constitution. Upon the designation of Pell City, Walter Chamberlin produced the plans and Robert Manley contracted to build the new courthouse. Chamberlin's simple rectangular plan is much more like his Covington County courthouse (*q.v.*) than his larger buildings in Crenshaw, Dallas, DeKalb, Lamar, Morgan, Tallapoosa or Walker counties (*q.v.*). In November 1902, as the building was rising, the local train station caught fire, and when the townspeople gathered to watch the spectacle, cases of dynamite inside exploded, killing some, injuring many, and damaging a number of buildings, including the unfinished courthouse. By March 1903, the damage was repaired, the building was finished, and the County Court accepted it.

The horizontal emphasis that Chamberlin produced with water table, repeating segmental window arches, unadorned eave line and shallow hipped roof, was an effective contrast to the vertical emphasis of the unusual entrance bay, rising from the stepped enframement of a deeply recessed arched portal through a decorative window frame and more stepped brickwork to the short belfry above the roof line. Some of this effect has, disappointingly, been lost by later alterations.

St. Clair County Courthouse, Ashville (1845, '86; 1911, '38–39)

(1845, 1886) Architect: Unrecorded; Builder: Littleton Yarbrough

The first brick courthouse in St. Clair County was the middle section of the building pictured at top on the facing page. With a similar history, it bears comparison with the nearby 1854 Shelby County courthouse. Littleton Yarbrough (or Yarborough), a prominent county citizen, was the contractor and left a detailed record of the building project. The courthouse was a quite plain, square building with hipped roof supporting a square bell tower. Inside was the usual arrangement of four offices below and courtroom above. As can be seen from the upper photograph, the windows of the original section had 12-over-12-light sash. The front entrance section and the rear section were added in 1886, the windows there having 8-over-8 sash.

In the lower photograph on the facing page, dated about 1900, of a group posing, the mass of the whole building can be understood somewhat more clearly.

(1911, 1938–39) Architect: Unrecorded; Builder: Unrecorded

The St. Clair County courthouse in Ashville has been altered many times. Its appearance in 2015 (above), with monumental classical portico, was by and large the result of the 1911 remodeling of the 1886 building (facing page, bottom) that was itself an expansion of the 1845 building (facing page, top). The building also underwent a major renovation in 1938–39 through a grant from the New Deal-era Works Progress Administration.

Arrington Collection, Julia Tutwiler Library, University of West Alabama

SUMTER COUNTY COURTHOUSE, LIVINGSTON (1839)

Architect: Unrecorded; Builder: Theodore Spence

Unlike the usual sequence of courthouse buildings in Alabama counties (*i.e.*, log-frame-brick), in Sumter the original log courthouse was succeeded by a brick courthouse. When the foundations of that building failed, a frame courthouse replaced it in 1839. The only known photograph of the 1839 courthouse is that above, picturing a group of men standing in front of the building (at right), displaying the results of a rabbit hunt. It occupied the same town square where its predecessor stood and its 1902 successor now stands. The frame 1839 courthouse burned in 1901.

Except that it has two stories, the image is too indistinct to display other features of the courthouse. Fortunately, specifications for the building have been preserved, which, assuming they were followed as written, allows a greater understanding of the building. The upper floor of the 40' x 60' building was devoted to the courtroom, as usual. Jury rooms, however, were located on the lower floor, accessed from courtroom jury boxes by stairs. The lower floor was divided into four parts by one passage from the front door to a cross passage. Rooms opening into the cross passage were divided by a framed partition. A pair of staircases rising on both sides of the front door permitted access to the courtroom above.

While the building sides were given standard weatherboard treatment, specifications paid particularly detailed attention to the structural components of the frame. Though the roof probably was hipped, the description from the county commissioners includes this requirement: "The roof of the new House to form a comb in the centre for some 16 or 20 feet." Whether "comb" refers to a belfry or some other feature is unknown. The building to the left in the photograph was built in 1881 as the probate judge's office.

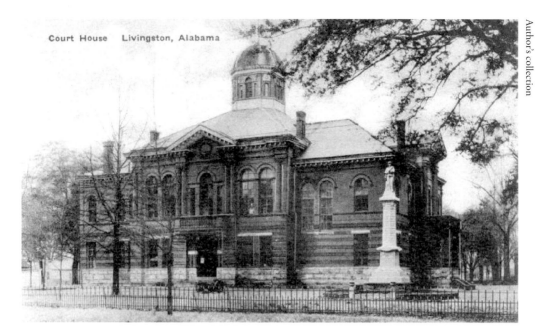

Court House Livingston, Alabama

Author's collection

SUMTER COUNTY COURTHOUSE, LIVINGSTON (1903)

Architect: Ausfeld & Chapman; Builder: C. H. Dabbs & Company

With several different partners, architect Frederick Ausfeld of Montgomery designed numbers of public buildings in Tennessee, Alabama (including Sidney Lanier High School), and
Florida. When the small frame courthouse on the square in Livingston burned in 1901,
Sumter County was ready to consolidate the collection of buildings that housed county
offices and court facilities into a proper courthouse befitting a cotton-prosperous town that
was a cultural and education center. Some of its gloss may have faded, but the Livingston
State College (now the University of West Alabama) and the courthouse remain to attest to
what once was, still is, and might be again.

Ausfeld's essentially Neo-Renaissance building is an imaginative combination of materials
and patterns—a rusticated stone base up to first-floor window sills, courses of brick alternating
with fanciful terra cotta bands up to second-floor level, wide belt course of brick to second-
floor window sills, a second story of plainly laid brick into which are set tall arched windows,
and finally a heavily modillioned cornice all around. Projecting bays on three of the four
elevations are enriched with paired columns, pediments, balcony, and a Palladian window
on the front and rear; the west entrance, but not the east, is a simpler version of the front
and rear. Capping the tall pitched roof, a domed cupola echoes in small scale the elements
below. All in all, a *tour de force* of a sort, built by the experienced Charles H. Dabbs from
nearby Meridian, Mississippi, also builder of the Newton County courthouse in Mississippi.

Author's collection

Talladega County Courthouse, Talladega (1844, 1905)

Architect: Unrecorded (1844), H. K. Chapman (1905); Builders: Jacob D. Shelley & Robert K. Hampson (1844), R. W. [perhaps R. S.] West (1905)

Talladega County authorities have made many substantial alterations to their courthouse since 1844. The earliest known photographs of the building show the first, a wing added to one end of the building in 1905. In the photograph above, the original building is to the left and nearly obscured, but its mansard-roofed belfry towers above the addition in the foreground. The 1905 addition, designed by the Atlanta architect H. K. Chapman, was a startling "improvement" over the marginally more conventional appearance of the original building. No nearby precedent for the banded columns at the recessed entrance come readily to mind though reportedly they have 16th century Italian precedents, sometimes copied in sophisticated American buildings. Further originality is found in the columns' composite capitals, the second-floor balcony that projects beyond the columns, and the crown above them. Although many changes have been made to the building since 1905, the distinctive columns remain.

TALLAPOOSA COUNTY COURTHOUSE, DADEVILLE (1839)

Architect: Unrecorded; Builders: Joshua S. Mitchell & Benjamin H. Cameron

Although no photograph of the earliest Tallapoosa County courthouse is known, this drawing appeared on a map of Dadeville in the 1830s. It is included here because of the connection between the Tallapoosa courthouse and the courthouses of Dallas County at Cahawba and Chambers County at LaFayette, all of which are attributed to the Troup County, Georgia, builder Joshua Mitchell and are of similar design to the courthouse he built there.

The color drawing shows white trim against red brick walls and above the doors semi-elliptical transoms emphasized by the lunette of the same shape in the pediment. The pediment is exactly the same as that in Chambers County, both spanning three central bays. Altogether, the elements comprise a neat Federal-style composition.

University of Alabama

John P. Oliver II

TALLAPOOSA COUNTY COURTHOUSE, DADEVILLE (1861)

Architect: Unrecorded; Builder: P. Coniff

Excepting only the Lowndes County courthouse (*q.v.*), the Tallapoosa County courthouse of 1861 may have been the purest South Carolina type "open arms" courthouse in Alabama. Each architectural detail in this Tuscan style rural courthouse, except the brackets under the eaves, is just what Thomas Jefferson approved in rustic public buildings. We know nothing about Coniff (or Conniff), the builder—not whether he built to his own design or to that of the county commissioners, nor whether he had lived in South Carolina or Lowndes County—nothing at all thus far.

Just as the building was completed, the Civil War began. During the conflict and long afterwards attention was diverted from maintaining the courthouse properly so that by the end of the nineteenth century, when prospects for the county began to brighten, the condition of the building and the need for additional space argued for a new courthouse. The new, however, did not replace the old—the old courthouse disappeared within the walls of the new one (see *infra*).

Tallapoosa Historical Museum

Tallapoosa County Courthouse, Dadeville (1902)

Architect: Walter Chamberlin; Builder: W. R. Harper

Walter Chamberlin left no exterior trace of the earlier Tallapoosa County courthouse in his design for the 1902 successor that swallowed it up. The old courthouse became the shell of the large center section of the new, but the 1861 front became the back of the 1902 building. Wall surfaces and windows were reworked and office wings added to both sides. The position of the clock tower in front of the left wing as seen above was duplicated with a corresponding two-story structure behind the wing seen at the right.

Chamberlin did not resort to the cookie-cutter approach he used so often in designing courthouses. The Dadeville building had a certain factory look to it, but the clock tower reaching a hundred feet skyward made clear that this was no factory. Even as imposing as the courthouse was, however, it eventually did not meet the county's need for space, so in 1948 the county added a further large section to the left of the tower. Apparently, even that did not satisfy, for the county razed the building in 1958 and moved into a new, very ordinary courthouse on the same site in 1960.

Little is known of the 1902 contractor, W. R. Harper, except that he was also the contractor for another Chamberlin courthouse in the Morgan County, Tennessee, town of Wartburg.

Tallapoosa Historical Museum

TALLAPOOSA COUNTY COURTHOUSE, ALEXANDER CITY (1890)

Architect: Not Recorded; Builder: David McCullough

Even though the Alabama Legislature had chosen Dadeville to be the seat of Tallapoosa County and even though a stylish county courthouse had been built there, the city fathers of a growing and ambitious Alexander City, a few miles north of Dadeville, decided in 1889 that their town should have a courthouse of its own for occasional sessions of the county court. A building was duly erected and until 1902 it was periodically a venue for the county court and regularly for a variety of municipal functions. It is said that the courthouse was built with funds raised entirely from private donations from community citizens.

David McCullough, an Opelika rock mason according to the 1880 U.S. Census, was awarded the contract for the stonework of which this, the first Alexander City courthouse, was built. As McCullough would have been about seventy-six when taking on the job, he must have been assisted by a substantial crew. The photograph shows the building in 1899, after it had stood about nine years, fitted out with prominent brackets under the eaves of a hipped roof. Asymmetrical placement of the flues piercing the roof make problematic the drawing of conclusions about interior arrangements.

Disaster struck the building and nearly all the buildings in Alexander City in 1902 when a devastating fire swept through the town and destroyed most of its buildings, including the recently organized Alexander City Cotton Mill. The mill was immediately rebuilt, later to become an Avondale Mill. The city authorities determined that the courthouse must also be rebuilt quickly.

An experienced Arizona architect recently transplanted to Birmingham, James M. Creighton, had come to Alexander City in search of design opportunities (one hotel was replaced from his designs). The minutes of the city's Common Council record that he submitted a sketch, "showing a brick wall of 2 inches to be built around the old rock walls as they stood to the best advantage as this was the most practical way that presented itself to the board as this would give considerable strength and appearance to the building." In the end, however, Creighton's suggestion was abandoned. Local historians record that "the smoked ruins of the courthouse were removed by dynamite," and the second Alexander City courthouse was erected on the same site, though not in quite so stylish a form.

Tallapoosa Historical Museum

TALLAPOOSA COUNTY COURTHOUSE, ALEXANDER CITY (1902)

Designer: Unrecorded; Builder: Unrecorded

In view of the disaster that destroyed the first Alex City Courthouse, city authorities again chose to build the second in masonry, presumably with some additional protection against fire. Notwithstanding the vertical bands worked out in the brick, the semi-circular transom above the front door, and the flattened brackets under the eaves, the building, so far as old photographs show us, does not exert the presence or stylishness of its predecessor. That is perhaps due in part to the orientation of the building, short façade to the street rather than longer side forward.

Yet it would be fair to credit the building with greater attention to comfort inside than in the first courthouse, for the elaborate chimney stacks show that the interior spaces must have been more easily warmed in cool weather than were such spaces in the older building. While neither the architect nor the builder of this second courthouse has yet been identified, when the city council advertised for bids from contractors, it did record the range of those it received—from $4,300 to $9,000—a range so great that the council avoided the responsibility by agreeing to have "the mayor talk with the different contractors and . . . let the contract for rebuilding of Court House to the best advantage."

In 1939 the second Alex City Courthouse was replaced on the same site by a third, WPA-financed project.

TUSCALOOSA COUNTY COURTHOUSE, TUSCALOOSA (1831, 1845)

Architect: Unrecorded; Builder: Unrecorded

The drawing above shows the second Tuscaloosa County courthouse as pictured on a birds-eye panoramic view of Tuscaloosa. Although built to be a Masonic Hall, the building was acquired by Tuscaloosa County in 1845 and served as its courthouse until 1908 when the county administration moved to the building pictured next (*infra*). County records show that in 1846 the city of Tuscaloosa built the clock tower and retained ownership of it even after the county administration departed the building.

Tuscaloosa County Court House. TUSCALOOSA, Ala.

Keith Vincent, *Courthouse History*

Tuscaloosa County Courthouse, Tuscaloosa (1908)

Architect: William Ernest Spink; Builder: Carrigan & Lynn Construction Co.

Having once been the capital city of Alabama (1826–46) and therefore accustomed to grand civic buildings, Tuscaloosa County has been more attentive than most to matters concerning its courthouse. Perhaps then it is no surprise that seven different buildings served the county as its courthouse during Tuscaloosa's first ninety years, and this, the seventh, was the grandest. It was a fine classical building designed by William E. Spink, who had come to Birmingham from Indiana as a young man. In Alabama he was known especially for his Colonial Revival work, of which the Tuscaloosa courthouse was typical. Later he moved to New Orleans.

Also from Birmingham were the builders, C. O. Lynn and J. C. Carrigan. At a cost publicized as $100,000, they provided Tuscaloosa a very up-to-date facility. The principal eastern entrance opened onto a broad corridor that ran the length of the first floor and along which were the county's administrative offices. On the second floor, as usual, was the courtroom, here with wire-glass skylights. The building was also up-to-date in having a central steam heating system and what appears to have been a fire extinguishing system that ran 50' vertical pipes outfitted with 2½" hoses from the basement through both floors.

Birmingham Public Library

WALKER COUNTY COURTHOUSE, JASPER (1886)

Architect: Unrecorded; Builders: Shields & Wilson

After three previous courthouses were lost to war and fires, Walker County managed to conduct county business continuously in this building until 1907 when another replaced it. The boxy mass of the structure gave it an air of simplicity, an impression not diluted by the decorative hood molds above the windows and door, pilasters, paired brackets at the eaves, and balcony.

Court House and Monument, Jasper, Ala.

WALKER COUNTY COURTHOUSE, JASPER (1908)

Architect: Walter Chamberlin; Builder: B. C. Bynum

Walter Chamberlin could design a conventional neoclassical courthouse as well as any of his competitors on the Alabama courthouse scene. Hardly anything could be complained about in his 1908 Walker County courthouse in Jasper, unless it is the unusually tall plinths supporting the portico columns. As a consequence, the columns do not appear as robust as the grand porticoes on three sides of the building require. Chamberlin, it must be said, was not an architect to insist that everything about a courthouse be unique. While the clock tower in Jasper is not so identifiable a composition as his clock towers in Luverne or Selma, it is, nonetheless one that he duplicated in other courthouses—in Scotland County, Missouri, and Marion County, Florida, for example. Bynum, the contractor, was an experienced Birmingham builder, who worked with a very different Chamberlin design in Lamar County (*q.v.*)

The 1908 Walker County courthouse was greatly admired for its setting, in a formal park-like landscape design. However, as so many other courthouses had been, this one was a fire casualty, notwithstanding its designation as "fireproof" by both the builder and the Sanborn Fire Insurance Map Company. The foundations of this building lived on, however, to serve as a base for the succeeding 1933 courthouse.

WASHINGTON COUNTY COURTHOUSE, ST. STEPHENS (1854)

Architect: Unrecorded; Builder: Levin Jefferson Wilson

Against all odds, the frame 1854 Washington County courthouse still stands. Unlike so many other vintage Alabama courthouses, neither fire nor neglect has brought it down. Moreover, now carefully restored, it still occupies its original site. As pointed out previously, a number of the earlier Alabama courthouses separated their administrative and judicial functions by placing the former on the ground floor and the latter on the second, providing a separate entrance to the second floor from outside the building. That arrangement was used at St. Stephens to particular effect, becoming the principal design feature of the building. In part the effect is possible because the stairs are not obscured by columns under the pediment that is supported by slender posts. The National Register nomination for the building, however, asserts: "The double exterior stair . . . no doubt is a later addition, as the original function of the building as a Court House does not seem to suggest the use of stairs for purposes of a court house." (The old Masonic Hall in Perry County and the Tuckahatchee Masonic Hall in Russell County employed the porch-and-stairs arrangement found in the Washington County courthouse, so perhaps the feature appealed for both political and fraternal purposes.)

The builder of the courthouse, and a nearby church, was Levin Jefferson Wilson, who came from Maryland to Alabama about ten years after it had become a state. He prospered, apparently by virtue of large landholdings. In the 1860 U.S. Census, his occupation was "Farmer," and the value of his real estate was $50,000 and of personal property $126,000, indicating that he was a substantial slaveholder. These facts make it probable that he was not the builder in the literal sense, but was the supervisor of construction that perhaps was done by his bondsmen.

Keith Vincent, *CourthouseHistory*

WASHINGTON COUNTY COURTHOUSE, CHATOM (1908)

Architect: W. S. Hull; Builder: Southern Structural Steel Co.

In 1907 Washington County voters chose to move the county seat from "new" St. Stephens to the more centrally located Chatom. Washington County officials paid the Mississippi architect W. S. Hull $1,650 for designing its 1908 courthouse at Chatom. One cannot help wondering why—for Hull had presented the same design to officials in in the adjoining Choctaw County for their 1906 courthouse. Despite the oddity of this circumstance, in both cases the result was a handsome building, and no recorded public dismay arose over the twin next door. An especially smooth appearance of the exterior surfaces, both here and in Choctaw County, was achieved by using pressed brick with color-matching mortar joints. No explanation remains for either the square or the pedimented dormers (unseen but matched on the far side of the building) on the roof. In the renovated Choctaw courthouse, the dormers, now louvered, are part of the HVAC system.

The contractor, the Southern Structural Steel Co., was a San Antonio, Texas, firm that had established itself as a builder of jails and fireproof records vaults, so it was an easy expansion to extend its territory into Arkansas, Alabama, and Georgia and its repertoire into courthouses. Their contract for this building amounted to $9,000, which the *Manufacturers' Record* reported included "brick and stone construction; fireproof; 32.6 x 35.1 feet; hot-air heating plant; slate roof . . . considerable quantities of limestone, terrazzo, marble tile, steel, cement and slate." For an additional unannounced sum, the company also built a new jail.

Keith Vincent, *CourthouseHistory*

CAMDEN'S COURT HOUSE

WILCOX COUNTY COURTHOUSE, CAMDEN (1859)

Architect and Builder: Alexander J. Bragg

A fortunate survivor for a century and a half is Camden's Wilcox County courthouse. It was designed and built by Alexander Jackson Bragg, who had come to the county from Warrenton, North Carolina, about 1840 and provided the county and the state a number of finely designed and constructed buildings. Except for the brackets under the eaves, fashionable at the time, the courthouse is in classic Greek Revival style, in this case using fluted Doric columns. Some have speculated that the exterior iron stairs to the second-floor courtroom were not part of the original design in which stairs were inside the building but were added in the 1880s. The question is still open; settling it would have to include some explanation of the absence of windows across the first floor of the façade. The date of this photograph is uncertain, but the board fence would have been an early feature necessary to keep free-ranging livestock away from the building. Moreover, the window shutters seen here are no longer seen in photographs at least as early as the 1930s.

The courthouse has been more fortunate than most in additions made to it. The 1959 wings added to both sides were a successful complement to the original style. Although the current county courthouse is now a modern building some distance from the old courthouse, the county still maintains some offices on its ground floor and the county library on the second.

Winston County Courthouse, Double Springs (1894)

Architect and Builder: Andrew Jackson Ingle

The coursed-rubble sandstone courthouse for Winston County that A. J. Ingle built in Double Springs in 1894 was a quite ordinary building, with some impressive qualities. Its well-laid rough surfaces of local sandstone give an impression of strength and permanence that in a smaller building might seem only picturesque or charming. It also seems to have been thoughtfully sited so that the building appeared to sit on a platform above grade, an impression emphasized by the prominent water table around the building. The principal façade that we see in this photograph requires some study. The entrance door is the only opening for the first floor. If offices were to the left and right of the entrance, the builder would have let in windows rather than leaving those walls solid. Most likely then, stairs both left and right of the door rose to a second-floor courtroom. The staircases may have been inside but, just as likely, this is another case where the courtroom was entered from outside rather than through the first floor. Where a balcony appears in the photograph would then have been a stair landing from which one entered to the rear of the courtroom. No records explain how the balcony was used, or if it was (cf., courthouses for Barbour and Wilcox counties). The one-story rear section of the building that can be seen in this photograph was a subsequent addition of uncertain purpose (possibly a jail) or date (possibly 1911).

Andrew Jackson Ingle was identified in censuses as a merchant before the Civil War. He claimed personal property valued at $4,400 in 1860. In the 1870 census, the value of his personal property had declined to $2,000 although the value of his real estate had increased. It seems likely, therefore, that he had been at least a minor slaveholder before the war.

A Last Word

Although a collection of early photographs of Alabama's older courthouses may be of considerable antiquarian interest, the author hopes to serve other purposes as well. Perhaps readers will bring to light other courthouse photographs that have escaped this author's detection so that a more complete collection of these images can be made available to the public.

If, in addition, a collection of their images encourages a more general consideration of Alabama courthouses than has heretofore been available, that would be a valuable development as well. Numbers of studies of individual courthouses have been written for appreciative local audiences; few studies treat the subject of Alabama courthouses generally. In 1966, the National Society of the Colonial Dames of America in the State of Alabama published the first collection of Alabama courthouse materials and images, *Early Courthouses of Alabama Prior to 1860.* Though it was not comprehensive, it was a useful beginning. Except for a recent picture book of extant courthouses in Alabama, the only other study is the collection of articles, "Building Alabama's Courthouses," by Samuel Rumore that appeared in *The Alabama Lawyer* between 1987 and 1996. In those essays, some descriptive material about courthouses in each county is presented along with a detailed history of the county as a political jurisdiction. Granting that a general study of everything worth saying about Alabama courthouses would be a valuable exercise, no existing study, including this one, has done that. The images and the information accompanying them here may provide a preliminary step for such works.

As suggested above concerning the Lauderdale County courthouse, C. Vann Woodward's *Origins of the New South, 1877–1913* expressed skepticism that taste and resources in the postbellum South were up to the challenge of building architecturally significant structures. The stories of courthouse history promise a test of Woodward's generalization about the availability of resources and the standards of taste in Alabama. Another student of the region, the trenchant W. J. Cash, argued in *The Mind of the South* that the personal- and the social-psychology in the South was little different in the New South than in the Old South. So what might courthouses tell us about that? Quite a lot, it seems. If Cash is right, some of the stories that Alabama courthouses tell would vary little over the first century and yet another stretch of years beyond that in the history of the state. Or perhaps these stories can tell us how and why that came to be, if it did—not only that designs and sizes and locations, for instance, might or might not fundamentally change over time, but how their designs and sizes and locations were chosen and influenced might or might not have changed.

The built environment, in which for a long time the county courthouse dominated the landscape, particularly in rural counties, is a useful emblem of elements of social history such as wealth, taste, social status, political power, and the relationships among them, along with the state of building technology. Courthouses are in one way unlike many other building types. Not only are they for a whole community, in a sense they are by a whole community. The county legal authority may decide who, what, where, when about courthouse projects, but their decisions are, both directly and indirectly, strongly influenced by the electorate, indeed by the whole community's sense of what is fitting, what is economical, what is convenient, what is handsome, and what is effective. Referenda may decide where a courthouse is placed and whether a bond issue will finance the costs. Elections have, in fact, turned on courthouse decisions made by county commissions and probate judges in considering whether to retain county officials in office or turn them out. The Covington County Board of Revenue election of 1914 is a good example.

In contrast, the decision of the householder determines what a house should be (at least before zoning became widespread). What a church is to be depends on the congregation; a school on educational experts and a board of education; a hospital on the local medical association. In such cases, the community at large defers to the preferences of special or expert decision makers. But the courthouse—in the years before courthouses became merely unremarkable office blocks—incorporated the influence and character of the whole county, even in those times when a segment of the community was excluded from full participation in its life.

One has only to examine any recent general history of Alabama to find that little attention is paid to the integral part of the common culture played by architectural preference and accomplishment. Individual buildings are celebrated sometimes and individual architects occasionally; courthouses, seldom. As a marker for the character of a whole community, the record of early courthouses is too valuable for general historical understanding to be ignored.

Index

All counties and cities are in Alabama unless otherwise indicated.

Lost Auburn

A VILLAGE REMEMBERED IN PERIOD PHOTOGRAPHS

by Ralph Draughon Jr., Delos Hughes, and Ann Pearson

Lost Auburn includes more than two hundred photographs of Auburn's buildings—lost to natural disaster, war, poverty, neglect, and "progress"—together with the stories of those who once worshipped, learned, and lived in Auburn.

Together, these photographs and the accompanying text—written by historians Ralph Draughon Jr., Delos Hughes, and Ann Pearson—vividly convey the uniqueness of the village of Auburn that was.

"*Lost Auburn* is a unique history of the town and university which describes in loving specificity the many people and places that make Auburn special."

— DAN BENNETT, Dean Emeritus,
Auburn University College of Architecture

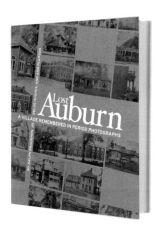

ISBN 978-1-60306-119-3
Trade Cloth, 184 pages, $29.95
7.625 x 9.25

*Available from your
favorite bookstore or visit
www.newsouthbooks.com/lostauburn*

ANCHORS *of* FAITH

Early Wooden Churches of the Deep South

MARTHA LEE DICKSON

Martha Dickson's *Anchors of Faith* gives a pictorial overview of 145 late-nineteenth century wooden churches located in southern Alabama, Mississippi, and throughout Florida. The author's descriptions and photos detail information about both the architecture of these houses of worship and their related histories. From Greek Revival to Victorian Gothic, Dickson helps add to the understanding of religious faith in the rural South through the architecture and history of its churches.

"A memorable overview of historic church architecture."
— DOUG PURCELL, Executive Director Emeritus,
Historic Chattahoochee Commission

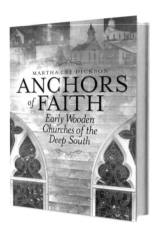

ISBN 978-1-60306-311-1
Trade Paper, 200 pages, $27.95
7 x 10

*Available from your
favorite bookstore or visit
www.newsouthbooks.com/anchorsoffaith*

Eugene Allen Smith's *Alabama*
by Aileen Kilgore Henderson

In the late 1800s, Alabama State Geologist Eugene Allen Smith braved chills, fevers, and verbal abuse as he searched for industrial raw materials that could bring about better lives for destitute Alabamians. What he accomplished transformed Alabama from an aimless and poverty-stricken agricultural state to an industrial giant to be reckoned with. The story of "Little Doc," as told in *Eugene Allen Smith's Alabama*, is drawn from many sources including Smith's transcribed field notes and his published reports over a period of fifty years.

"*Eugene Allen Smith's Alabama* reintroduces a preeminent Alabamian who had a positive influence in shaping his native state and who left an enduring legacy of science and service."
— LEWIS DEAN, Geological Survey of Alabama

ISBN 978-1-58838-243-6
Trade Cloth, 272 pages, $34.95
7.625 x 9.25

*Available from your
favorite bookstore or visit
www.newsouthbooks.com/eugenesmith*

Through a WOMAN'S EYE

The Early 20th Century Photography of Alabama's Edith Morgan

Through a Woman's Eye presents an evocative collection of a hundred black and white photographs made by Edith Morgan of Camden, a small town in Wilcox County, Alabama, just after the turn of the twentieth century. Morgan was educated locally before attending the School of the Chicago Art Institute. Subsequently she returned to Camden where she spent the remainder of her life teaching art.

This volume collects Morgan's photographs, along with essays by photographer Marian Furman and Professor Hardy Jackson that put them in the context of time and place. Dr. Matthew Mason of Yale's Beinecke Rare Book and Manuscript Library presents additional biographical information and offers a critical assessment of Morgan's photographs, comparing her work to that of contemporary photographers.

ISBN 978-1-58838-263-4
Trade Cloth, 160 pages, $29.95
8 x 9

*Available from your
favorite bookstore or visit
www.newsouthbooks.com/edithmorgan*